T0123382

The
Covering
and The
Light

TEENA HALL

WESTBOW
PRESS®
A DIVISION OF THOMAS NELSON
& ZONDERVAN

Copyright © 2016 Teena Hall.

Author Photo by Adam Bailey

All rights reserved. No part of this book may be used or reproduced by any means, graphic, electronic, or mechanical, including photocopying, recording, taping or by any information storage retrieval system without the written permission of the author except in the case of brief quotations embodied in critical articles and reviews.

Scripture taken from the Holy Bible, NEW INTERNATIONAL VERSION®. Copyright © 1973, 1978, 1984, 2011 by Biblica, Inc. All rights reserved worldwide. Used by permission. NEW INTERNATIONAL VERSION® and NIV® are registered trademarks of Biblica, Inc. Use of either trademark for the offering of goods or services requires the prior written consent of Biblica US, Inc.

WestBow Press books may be ordered through booksellers or by contacting:

WestBow Press
A Division of Thomas Nelson & Zondervan
1663 Liberty Drive
Bloomington, IN 47403
www.westbowpress.com
1 (866) 928-1240

Because of the dynamic nature of the Internet, any web addresses or links contained in this book may have changed since publication and may no longer be valid. The views expressed in this work are solely those of the author and do not necessarily reflect the views of the publisher, and the publisher hereby disclaims any responsibility for them.

Any people depicted in stock imagery provided by Thinkstock are models, and such images are being used for illustrative purposes only. Certain stock imagery © Thinkstock.

ISBN: 978-1-5127-4497-2 (sc)
ISBN: 978-1-5127-4498-9 (hc)
ISBN: 978-1-5127-4496-5 (e)

Library of Congress Control Number: 2016909338

Print information available on the last page.

WestBow Press rev. date: 06/27/2016

DAY 1

God has you covered, like the water covers the rocks that stay close. The rocks that are too far away are dry as bone.

> Blessed is the one whose transgressions are forgiven, whose sins are covered. Blessed is the one whose sin the Lord does not count against them... (Psalm 32:1–2)

You lose the light when you wander into deep waters. When you pull yourself out of the deep, you will find the light still there; but you must pull yourself to the light.

> The night is nearly over; the day is almost here. So let us put aside the deeds of darkness and put on the armor of light. (Romans 13:12)

DAY

3

Be with the waves, and be with God. God is like the waves washing over you; he is like the wind, he is like the sun—like the light and the warmth. God is like the waves. You are in God and God is in you!

> Don't you know that you yourselves are God's temple and that God's Spirit dwells in your midst? (1 Corinthians 3:16)

DAY 4

You linger with God, and he will linger with you. Take note, God is everywhere. Include him in everything. Start your day with God in the inner court, and then linger. That is intimacy.

> Come near to God and he will come near to you. Wash your hands, you sinners, and purify your hearts, you double-minded. (James 4:8)

DAY
5

Keep making yourself available. Continue to place yourself in God's presence, and the anointing will wash over you in waves. Keep coming back for filling up, because although the tide may be high now it goes to low tide and dries up. You must return again and again, for fresh anointing.

> Restore to me the joy of your salvation and grant me a
> willing spirit, to sustain me. (Psalm 51:12)

DAY
6

God is always talking to you, if you would but listen. Listen intently, as if your life depends on it; because it does. Life everlasting!

> "Very truly I tell you, whoever hears my word and believes him who sent me has eternal life and will not be judged but has crossed over from death to life." (John 5:24)

DAY 7

Look to the clouds to be reminded of Christ ascending back into heaven. At the same time, remember that he is here. He is right here; just look for him.

> But as for me, I watch in hope for the Lord, I wait for God my Savior; my God will hear me. (Micah 7:7)

DAY

8

God's love will wash over you, wave upon wave upon wave. Just like the ocean. Sit with the Lord in silence; you will be as calm as the ocean when it is smooth as glass.

He says, "Be still, and know that I am God..." (Psalm 46:10)

DAY
9

Although it is raining, the sun will come back—just like the Son of God will come back. Fix yourself on Jesus and the Father; bask in their love, and rejoice that you will soon be reunited with Christ!

> "Let us acknowledge the Lord; let us press on to acknowledge him. As surely as the sun rises, he will appear; he will come to us like the winter rains..." (Hosea 6:3)

DAY

10

God's love for you is like the never ceasing waves in the ocean; it is so vast! God's love is like the clouds in the sky, it is like the chirping of birds, it is like the blades of grass. God's love is like the breeze, blowing through the wheat fields. It is just that vast.

> But because of his great love for us, God, who is rich in mercy, made us alive with Christ even when we were dead in transgressions—it is by grace you have been saved. (Ephesians 2:4–5)

DAY 11

Though you could easily get lost in the vastness of this place, you are well known to God. Though there are millions and trillions of waves and clouds, he knows them all. You are only lost when you choose to be. Remember, God knew you before time began.

> The gatekeeper opens the gate for him, and the sheep listen to his voice. He calls his own sheep by name...
> (John 10:3)

DAY 12

Be still, and feel the peace of being one with God. Rest in him, all the days of your life—that is the only way to master the art of living in this world. Until you are reunited with the Lord, it is your only recourse.

> I delight greatly in the Lord; my soul rejoices in my God. For he has clothed me with garments of salvation and arrayed me in a robe of his righteousness, as a bridegroom adorns his head like a priest, and as a bride adorns herself with her jewels. (Isaiah 61:10)

DAY

13

Remember God in everything you do; put him first. You will see your life changing, right before your eyes, and you will receive favor from man. More importantly, you will honor God, truly honor God!

> Glorify the Lord with me; let us exalt his name together.
> (Psalm 34:3)

DAY

14

Watch nature, to learn. The animals work as a team, when they must; they practice patience and they do not worry or fret. They stay in the moment; they trust their Father completely. They show humility, and they are joyful. Just watch to learn.

> This is what I have observed to be good: that it is appropriate for a person to eat, to drink and to find satisfaction in their toilsome labor under the sun during the few days of life God has given them—
> (Ecclesiastes 5:18)

DAY
15

Sit and be with God early; stay with him for the day. Watch what happens—you will gain wisdom, you will have peace, and this will change your life. It is your choice; just wait and see what God does in you, and through you.

> I give them eternal life, and they shall never perish; no one will snatch them out of my hand. (John 10:28)

DAY

16

Focus on God; focus on praise and worship. Block out the static of the world; it will always be there. You must take authority. Let the chaff fall where it may. You are wheat.

> "When the Son of man comes in his glory, and all the angels with him, he will sit on his glorious throne. All the nations will be gathered before him, and he will separate the people one from another as a shepherd separates the sheep from the goats." (Matthew 25:31–32)

DAY

17

Listen to God. He will speak to you. Obey him and God will direct you. Look to God; he will guide you to the path he laid out for you. Only you. Before time began.

> Your eyes saw my unformed body; all the days ordained for me were written in your book before one of them came to be. (Psalm 139:16)

Sun with cloud cover

DAY

18

Stop, listen and obey. Turn off your mind. Relax into the Lord; he will feed you what you need. Stay fixed on the Lord. He will fill you up with his unconditional love!

> May the God of hope fill you with all joy and peace as you trust in him, so that you may overflow with hope by the power of the Holy Spirit. (Romans 15:13)

DAY

19

God is here, he is right here—feel his love in the breeze, and hear his assurances in the sounds of nature. Close your eyes, meditate on him, and know that he is God.

> The Lord is exalted over all the nations, his glory above
> the heavens. (Psalm 113:4)

DAY
20

Relax in knowing that God has you covered. God has the best things for you, as long as you stay the course. Do not deviate. You will be blessed.

> Lord, who may dwell in your sacred tent? Who may live on your holy mountain? The one whose walk is blameless, who does what is righteous, who speaks the truth from their heart... (Psalm 15:1–2)

DAY
21

Wait to hear God's voice; intently listen. Block out the world, each and every day, in order to hear what God has for you. He will give you marching orders. You need them more than ever now. Know that God loves you!

> Jesus replied, "Anyone who loves me will obey my teaching. My Father will love them, and we will come to them and make our home with them." (John 14:23)

DAY

22

The Lord will sustain you; rest your mind, knowing that you will not do without. Look to him, like a child does his parent, and ask for what you desire. Remember, he is (your daddy) Abba, your loving Father.

> Consider the ravens: They do now sow or reap, they have no storeroom or barn; yet God feeds them. (Luke 12:24)

DAY

23

Though you may get caught up in the undertow, if you trust and let go, God will help you drift ashore. Sometimes you have to go out to sea, with absolutely no control, because when you fully surrender God will bring you home. Just call out to him.

> For this reason, since the day we heard about you, we have not stopped praying for you. We continually ask God to fill you with the knowledge of his will through all the wisdom and understanding that the Spirit gives... (Colossians 1:9)

DAY
24

Listen for the Father's voice in the waves, listen for his voice in the bird's song, and listen for his voice in the cricket's chirp. Listen for the Father's voice in the breeze. God is everywhere. Avail yourself to him, and you will begin to recognize God in everything!

> God did this so that they would seek him and perhaps reach out for him and find him, though he is not far from any one of us. (Acts 17:27–28)

DAY

25

Remain obedient, and always be faithful to God. Stay on the narrow path; there are rewards. Hear God's commands, adhere to the lessons he will give specifically to you, and walk into enlightenment.

> A wicked person earns deceptive wages, but the one who
> sows righteousness reaps a sure reward. (Proverbs 11:18)

DAY
26

Know that he is God; know that he is good. Anything that is not light, is not from God and anything that is not good is not from him. Do not be deceived; look to the light to find God. You will not find him as long as you are lurking in shadows and darkness. Come into the light, to be in God's presence.

> "Listen to me, my people; hear me, my nation:
> Instruction will go out from me; my justice will become
> a light to the nations." (Isaiah 51:4)

DAY
27

Do not allow yourself feelings of defeat. When storms arrive, be still and listen for God's voice. He will shelter you and he will provide for you; he is at the helm. Let go and watch God shine!

> You have been a refuge for the poor, a refuge for the needy in their distress, a shelter from the storm and a shade from the heat. (Isaiah 25:4)

DAY 28

In the still, quiet softness, God is there. Though you cannot see him, he is near. Tune into God, and he will feed you. He will fulfill you, when you make a way to spend time with the Lord each day. Allow yourself to know God!

> And the peace of God, which transcends all understanding, will guard your hearts and your minds in Christ Jesus. (Philippians 4:7)

DAY

29

Let the breeze caress you, let the waves delight you; find your joy in loving the Lord. Find your peace in knowing that he will provide your every need. To understand God's power, and to understand his plans for you, surrender to him—body mind and spirit. Just listen for the voice of the Lord.

> "Yet if you devote your heart to him and stretch out your hands to him, if you put away the sin that is in your hand and allow no evil to dwell in your tent, then, free of fault, you will lift up your face; you will stand firm and without fear." (Job 11:13–15)

DAY

30

Relax into the day with no worries, knowing that God will take care of you. He has plans for you. Follow God and turn to him for counsel. You have already succeeded; you have overcome.

> You, dear children, are from God and have overcome them, because the one who is in you is greater than the one who is in the world. (1 John 4:4)

D A Y
31

Put your trust in God, and you will not fail. Do not look left or right; keep your focus on him. Stay fixed on righteousness, and ask for your Father's help. You are strong enough, and through him you will accomplish greatness.

> Blessed is the one who does not walk in step with the wicked or stand in the way that sinners take or sit in the company of mockers, but whose delight is in the law of the Lord, and who meditates on his law day and night. (Psalm 1:1–2)

DAY

32

Seek Christ, and get to know him. Go after goodness every day of your life. By doing this, you honor him. Better to know Jesus and die, than to be separated from him and live. Those who do not know Jesus Christ will die a second death. Those who know him, love him, honor him and follow him, have life everlasting!

> Multitudes who sleep in the dust of the earth will awake:
> some to everlasting life, others to shame and everlasting
> contempt. (Daniel 12:2)

DAY

33

Though you cannot see God, he is near. Envision his face to draw close to him. Listen for God's voice in the birdsong, in the winds and other sounds of nature. This will quiet your inner voice, making way for you to hear directly from God. Make this your daily practice. Connect with God first.

> But we ought always to thank God for you, brothers and sisters loved by the Lord, because God chose you as firstfruits to be saved through the sanctifying work of the Spirit and through belief in the truth. (2 Thessalonians 2:13)

D A Y

34

Be still with the breeze and be with the Lord, knowing that he will carry you where you need to go. Be tuned into the birds and you will hear from him. Feel the heavens above you and you will feel the Lord's unconditional love! Rest in nature and be content; you will always find rest in the Lord.

> Your love, Lord, reaches to the heavens, your faithfulness to the skies. Your righteousness is like the highest mountains, your justice like the great deep. (Psalm 36:5–6)

DAY
35

Do not waste valuable time on worry. Trust and believe that God will deliver you, Child. God has only good things in store for you.

> Every good and perfect gift is from above, coming down from the Father of the heavenly lights... (James 1:17)

What Satan meant for evil, God turned good and used it to glorify his kingdom. You can find rest in God's loving arms, and be enveloped in his peace; this is your choice.

> This is what the Lord says: "Stand at the crossroads and look; ask for the ancient paths, ask where the good way is, and walk in it..." (Jeremiah 6:16)

Mellow Sky

DAY

36

God treasures his time with you, Little One; it is as much for him as it is for you.

> For the Lord takes delight in his people; he crowns the
> humble with victory. (Psalm 149:4)

The world is dark, and getting darker; God wants his lights to come into his presence. This gladdens his heart. You do not know how important this is, how important you are. God sees you shining; you keep the fire lit. This happens when you continuously seek God's face!

> The fire must be kept burning on the altar continuously;
> it must not go out. (Leviticus 6:13)

DAY

37

Be obedient; in this you cannot fail. Obey God's commands—in the word, and individual commands, especially. This is how God will walk you into purpose, the divine purpose that you were anointed for before time began. You cannot dream, fantasize on, or imagine the works and rewards God has in store for you, Child. Be strong in faith, diligent and stay lit.

> Let love and faithfulness never leave you; bind them around your neck, write them on the tablet of your heart. (Proverbs 3:3)

DAY
38

Dream of what you want; tell God what you want. He is your Father
and he loves you. You will have more than you need: peace beyond
understanding, love like you have never known, and salvation, which
is more precious than all the jewels ever in the world. Tell God your
desires!

> This is the confidence we have in approaching God:
> that if we ask anything according to his will, he hears
> us. (1 John 5:14)

DAY 39

The Lord took you from wayward to onward; he took you from depressed and defeated, to joyful and hopeful. He took you out of the pit. You are already in the palace. Your worldly conditions do not matter; your spirit is what God loves. Do not look at your surroundings, look at your new beginnings. You have only just begun in your world, yet it is already finished.

> He has made everything beautiful in its time. He has also set eternity in the human heart; yet no one can fathom what God has done from beginning to end. (Ecclesiastes 3:11)

DAY
40

Boldly ask God for favor, believing that it is already done. Have faith in small matters, as well as big ones; you must exercise faith in everything. Your faith needs to be watered daily, to thrive. You will begin to expect favor, as a baby expects their every need to be met, and it is.

> May the favor of the Lord our God rest on us; establish
> the work of our hands for us— (Psalm 90:17)

Stop thinking. Just be. Be with God—no worries, no angst, no plans and no regrets. When you spend time just being with God, you feel his love outshining everything!

> Now may the Lord of peace himself give you peace at
> all times and in every way. (2 Thessalonians 3:16)

DAY 42

Depend on the Lord. Cherish your time with him, and you will develop a dependency on him. As you become accustomed to spending time with the Lord, you will find that your days are not complete lest you devote a portion of time for communing with him. He is your Father and he wants you to know him; to truly know him, you must prioritize a portion of your days to be alone with him. This is true intimacy, and it must be nurtured. Once this is a habit, you will be troubled if you cannot get this time alone with him. That is growth.

> My soul yearns, even faints, for the courts of the Lord;
> my heart and my flesh cry out for the living God. (Psalm
> 84:2)

DAY

43

Keep being with God, day after day after day. You will strengthen your walk, you will hear directly from the Lord, and you will no longer wander around aimlessly. You will soon know the plan that God has for your life; only then, can you walk into your divine purpose.

> "Now devote your heart and soul to seeking the Lord your God. Begin to build the sanctuary of the Lord God..." (1 Chronicles 22:19)

DAY

44

When you allow yourself to melt into God's presence, there is no room for anything else. You will then shake off worries, shake off insecurities, and you will shake off the "old man" ways. You have God's empowerment on you, like a mantle; do not take off the mantle.

> So Elijah went from there and found Elisha son of Shaphat. Elijah went up to him and threw his cloak around him. Elisha then left his oxen and ran after Elijah. Then he set out to follow Elijah and became his servant. (1 Kings 19:19, 20, 21)

DAY 45

You are never more alive, than when you are in God's presence. Live for these moments. Ask him to linger with you, every waking moment.

> And I will ask the Father, and he will give you another advocate to help you and be with you forever—the Spirit of truth. (John 14:16–17)

Now see how different your days, hours, and minutes are; you are a changed person. You now walk in enlightenment, illumination and light. Leave the darkness behind, where it belongs. Be lit and stay lit!

> Come, descendants of Jacob, let us walk in the light of the Lord. (Isaiah 2:5)

DAY 46

Do not fret. God knows the plans he has for each of you; do not get bogged down in other people's stuff. Focus on God; look above the mundane, look past the world, and know that God is measuring your steps. As long as you look to God only, for guidance and sustenance, you will be marching toward your God given destiny.

> The Lord is my shepherd, I lack nothing. He makes me lie down in green pastures, he leads me beside quiet waters, he refreshes my soul. (Psalm 23:1–3)

DAY
47

Anchor yourself in the Lord's love; you will find strength in this practice. Now, practice being one with him, daily. This will become a habit; make sure it is unbreakable. If you stay with this habit, the enormous lifestyle changes will be infinitely profound. Not only to you, other people will see vast changes too. You will grow much more grounded; it will take more and more to unsettle you, as you drift further and further into God's love. Things of the world take on much less importance. This is priceless.

> You were taught, with regard to your former way of life, to put off your old self, which is being corrupted by its deceitful desires; to be made new in the attitude of your minds; and to put on the new self, created to be like God in true righteousness and holiness. (Ephesians 4:22–24)

DAY

48

You need fresh fire daily to stay deeply rooted in God's love. By staying deeply rooted, you will not cave into the world's demands. Stay in the word; this keeps you in God's presence. By staying with God, you will not succumb to the enemy's wiles. Do not waste time focusing on the enemy's tricks. When you stay fixed on God and the word, you stay covered!

> These have come so that the proven genuineness of your faith—of greater worth than gold, which perishes even though refined by fire—may result in praise, glory and honor when Jesus Christ is revealed. (1 Peter 1:7)

DAY

49

Look to the Lord daily, for strength. When you look to him, first, you show faith in him. Without faith, nothing will manifest. God has a plan for your life, and it will not come to fruition until you completely surrender. You must leave childish ways behind, and you must place yourself in the Lord's hands; only you know when this has come to pass. Then watch what happens.

> For whoever wants to save their life will lose it, but whoever loses their life for me and for the gospel will save it. (Mark 8:35)

DAY

50

Infilling begins when you rest in the Lord. Put aside everything—
every thought and every deed. Nothing is more important than to fill
(yourself) up again and again, with the Holy Spirit. You will learn to
hear the good shepherd's voice, especially when you go off course; this
is crucial to your wellbeing. If you are emptied without daily refilling,
you miss out on the gifts of the Lord. You miss out on strengthening, and
you will be attacked in your weakness. Do not bring this upon yourself;
you must stay fixed on God, and you must be filling up constantly.

I keep my eyes always on the Lord. With him at my
right hand, I will not be shaken. (Psalm 16:8)

DAY

51

Remain unfazed by the happenings of the world, and stay fixed on God. Focus on his love for you, and share God's love with the world; there are lost souls that must be shown how to slough off the darkness. Every day, this is the task. Stay in the light, shed the darkness, and show the lost ones what true love is by walking, talking, being with God every waking moment. That is a testimony.

> But if we walk in the light, as he is in the light, we have
> fellowship with one another, and the blood of Jesus, his
> Son, purifies us from all sin. (1 John 1:7)

DAY

52

Seek God, meditate on God, rinse, repeat. Daily infilling happens by seeking God, first and foremost. You find him everywhere you look—in the wind, in the waves, in the skies, and on the page. Go into the word, each day, for God's intimate messages to you. Meditate on the word, and seek his face. God loves you, and you will feel his abundant love by doing this daily.

> I seek you with all my heart; do not let me stray from your commands. I have hidden your word in my heart that I might not sin against you. (Psalm 119:10–11)

Feel God's love, in the soothing ripples of water in the bay; sense his presence, in the sounds of the air, and recognize his hand, in the artwork scrolled across the wispy-clouded sky. Know that he is God, your Creator and Everlasting Father. Hear the waves, lapping the shore, and know that there is always more to drink in. Each day, you will have more of God's love to drink in. This well never runs dry.

> May the Lord make your love increase and overflow for each other and for everyone else, just as ours does for you. (1 Thessalonians 3:12)

Dark gray sky

DAY

54

Just be, like in nature—no struggles; things just happen. God gives peace, God gives strength, God gives endurance and God gives sustenance! Be at ease, await your assignment, and walk into it.

> Walk in obedience to all that the Lord your God has commanded you, so that you may live and prosper and prolong your days in the land that you will possess. (Deuteronomy 5:33)

DAY 55

God is here, just reach for him. He cares for your daily needs; give thanks to him. Do not take his love for granted. God does not like to take things away from you. You must be in the word for instruction, this keeps you focused on your Father. This keeps you faithful, and you will have much more joy in life. Remember to keep your eyes always fixed on your Father.

> Let your eyes look straight ahead; fix your gaze directly before you. (Proverbs 4:25)

DAY

56

If you want open heaven, share your love of God with the world. Show the world what it is to walk with him, daily. Show the lost what it is to truly know God. You do this by your demeanor. When you are one with God, you are at ease. When you walk with him, you have peace. When you linger with God, you exhibit true love!

> Whoever claims to live in him must live as Jesus did. (1 John 2:6)

DAY
57

When you learn to trust in God, you will feel safe; when you learn to walk with God, you will be safe. You need no other protection than God's covering. When you stop running to and fro, you will find him. Be still, listen for his voice, and you will hear from the Lord. This is the first sign of walking into the light.

> Whoever gives heed to instruction prospers, and blessed
> is the one who trusts in the Lord. (Proverbs 16:20)

DAY

58

Though you found comfort in the darkness, you cannot return to it. You were deceived into believing the darkness cloaked you in protection. When you live in darkness for seasons, the light at first hurts your eyes; you must adjust to the light, to find comfort in it. Once you bask in the light, for just a little while, you begin to thrive in the light. This is where you truly belong!

> For with you is the fountain of life; in your light we see light. (Psalm 36:9)

DAY
59

You flirted with the light, like the sunlight drips from the sky through a tree canopy above you in the forest. You took your time, meandering through the forest. You went off into caves, and other dark places, and you avoided coming out of the darkness. You need to run through the dancing light field. You need to hasten your pace, you need to recognize that time is of the essence and you must run to the light before it is too late!

> This is why it is said: "Wake up, sleeper, rise from the dead, and Christ will shine on you." (Ephesians 5:14)

DAY

60

Though you drifted far from shore, when you made your way home God was here. You were tossed about in the waves and the surf, and you were caught up in many riptides. What you learned, in the tumultuous sea, was different for each of you. But, now you know how to stay close to shore, where you are protected. Only God offers true shelter!

> For in the day of trouble he will keep me safe in his dwelling... (Psalm 27:5)

DAY
61

Even when storms roll in, it is calm on the horizon. You must weather the storm with patience and perseverance. Do not run from the storm; do not think you can master it either. Stay calm and keep a close eye on the storm; come to God for counsel. Listen very closely, and you will hear God's still, quiet voice. When you choose to listen to him, only then will you survive.

> He stilled the storm to a whisper; the waves of the sea were hushed. (Psalm 107:29)

DAY
62

It took a lifetime to get to this place; everything you have encountered, brought you precisely where you are today. You ran from God, you turned your back again and again; he caught you, and then he allowed you to jump back into stormy waters. You tried to be good in the world, you tried to "get by", you almost got away so many times. Now, he will not have you stripped away again. You are a child of God; you are his. Welcome home, Child; your work will soon begin. Completion is knocking!

> though he may stumble, he will not fall, for the Lord
> upholds him with his hand. (Psalm 37:24)

DAY 63

Wait patiently, for God to move you forward. The waves are gently swabbing the beach, wave after wave, never in a hurry; they just are. The waves have the reassurances of the winds, the constancy of tomorrow, and the promises of continuation. Patience.

He says, "Be still, and know that I am God..." (Psalm 46:10)

Fall into a routine, of beginning your days resting in God's loving arms. Know that he is God, and know that he has goodness planned for your life. Do not get sidetracked; stay on course, and God will reveal his plan for you. Just make yourself available. Listen closely for his voice, and walk obediently into your preordained, divine purpose.

> Submit yourselves, then, to God. Resist the devil, and
> he will flee from you. (James 4:7)

DAY
65

Though the winter can be cold and seems harsh, you are able to rest and recharge. The winter is a time for solitude. Some of the animals need to hibernate and they store up fat for winter, in preparation. They hole up for a while, and when they re-emerge, they are refreshed and reinvigorated. Use this time wisely, and prepare to do great things. You will marvel at what God does with you, once you are prepared.

> So then, let us not be like others, who are asleep, but let us be awake and sober. (1 Thessalonians 5:6)

DAY

66

Spring into the lovely, soft, sunshiny days with a joyful heart. Awakening, are the buds on the trees, and the world slowly is becoming vibrant again. The bird's song happily greets you in the mornings, as the days grow longer. Animals are waking up from long winter naps; they are breeding, and there is a newfound joy in the air. Excitement stirs, and renewal abounds; tap into this abundance, and be thankful that you are alive!

> May the God of hope fill you with all joy and peace as
> you trust in him… (Romans 15:13)

DAY
67

Summer is a time of harvest preparation; the fruits of your labor are soon to be realized, and the final stretch is at hand. You feel the sun beating on your neck, and you know that your hard work will soon pay off. Stick to the script God has given you; trust in him, and have faith that you are walking into the purpose for which you were created. Do not look left or right, or get off course; stay fixed on God, and he will lead you exactly where he wants you to be. Get ready to reap the rewards of a harvest that will overcome any fears you have of lack. You will soon have a surplus, and you will be able to shower others with abundance. You have a loving heart, and you will show others how to truly love their neighbors. Agape love is the purest!

> A sluggard's appetite is never filled, but the desires of the diligent are fully satisfied. (Proverbs 13:4)

DAY
68

Love flows like the waves, and peace careens in the winds. Walk into your purpose with the elegance of a bird, soaring through the air. Have the patience of a duck, floating on the water. Nature is in no hurry. Flora and fauna are not out to impress others. There is no competition in wildlife, only life, abundantly thriving. Look to God, and thrive. Know that he is here, God is right here—a heartbeat away!

> "I am the Alpha and the Omega," says the Lord God, "who is, and who was, and who is to come, the Almighty." (Revelation 1:8)

DAY

69

Be with God, all the livelong day. Love God. Know that you are loved and that you were created with purpose! Do not look at others, do not listen to naysayers, and do not tell others God's plans for you. Watch what happens, Little One. You keep your eyes, heart, soul and spirit fixed on the Lord. You belong to him.

> You are my strength, I watch for you; you, God, are my
> fortress... (Psalm 59:9)

DAY
70

Though the skies turn dark, you need not worry; the sun will return tomorrow. Keep your eyes turned up to the heavens, and stay in tune with the promises God has made to you. These can be claimed only when you are obedient. Love God with your entire being, love your neighbor as you love yourself. You will reap rewards when you achieve this level of existence, and sustain the enlightenment.

> For the entire law is fulfilled in keeping this one command: "Love your neighbor as yourself." (Galatians 5:14)

DAY
71

Enjoy the dusk and the dawn; watch renewal come over the earth. Listen to the sounds of the earth awakening. Smell the promises of a brand new day, and bask in the love God has beset upon the world, every place you look. Know that he is your living, loving Father. See what is in store for you, and marvel as the wonders abound.

Many, Lord my God, are the wonders you have done,
the things you planned for us. (Psalm 40:5)

Harvest is a time of joy, the time when your hard work—blood, sweat, and tears—pays off. It is a time to share the bounty, and watch others consume the fruits of your labor. Be grateful for abundance; be only too happy to provide for other people, as this is love.

> Give to the one who asks you, and do not turn away from
> the one who wants to borrow from you. (Matthew 5:42)

DAY

73

Be with God, constantly, and you will grow to know him. Worship, meditate, pray, study, and make smart choices in everything—the company you keep, what you see and what you hear; protect yourself, in all aspects of life. Beware of the enemy, he is a wolf in sheep's clothing; do not be fooled. Stay with God, and you will hear from him. The Lord will provide to you "ears that hear and eyes that see…" and he will show you how to gain understanding and discernment. You are his beloved child; always keep that first in your mind.

> The fear of the Lord leads to life; then one rests content, untouched by trouble. (Proverbs 19:23)

DAY
74

Pay attention to the sights and sounds of nature; God will communicate with you in this way. Seek him first, seek him daily, seek him constantly; seek him in all ways. You will know God better and better, each day that you do this. You will grow closer to him, you will grow stronger and you will be more prepared to walk into purpose. Begin with listening for God's soft, still voice and know that he is God—your Father, Abba, Redeemer, King of Kings, Prince of Peace.

> My heart says of you, "Seek his face!" Your face, Lord,
> I will seek. (Psalm 27:8)

In the last days there are times to act with urgency, like waves racing to shore. The sun still shines, warming them, but deep below the surface it is black as night. You will have to race as quickly as possible, to break the surface, and rush to the light. You must act fast, or risk losing the light. When you act with a sense of purpose and urgency, others will know the seriousness of getting to the light. They will then follow.

> For you once were darkness, but now you are light in the
> Lord. Live as children of light… (Ephesians 5:8)

Keep plodding forward, even when you do not feel like it. The waves in the ocean never take a break; they keep moving. When you do this, you take energy and place it in lightness; this makes very little room for darkness, and negativity leaking in becomes less likely. Stay in motion, and you stay the course. This enables God to direct you, straight into your purpose.

> Give careful thought to the paths for your feet and be steadfast in all your ways. (Proverbs 4:26)

DAY

77

By staying in God's presence, daily, you get rooted. The longer you continue this practice, the deeper the roots go. The deeper the roots, the stronger you grow. You become equipped for battle. Stand ready for battle at every moment; you are in warfare constantly. You begin to identify the enemy, even though he is disguised, and you will find adversaries where you least expect them. Be alert, and be discerning; resist the enemy. Keep your eyes on God.

> Be alert and of sober mind. Your enemy the devil prowls around like a roaring lion looking for someone to devour. (1 Peter 5:8)

DAY
78

Be still, and listen to God; he will instruct you each and every moment. Look to him for sustenance, in everything, and leave God out of nothing. You will honor him in this. Be patient, and the Lord will reveal his ministry for you. Do not get bogged down in other people's stuff. You work directly for God, and if it does not feel right in your spirit, it is not from him. Remember, the enemy shows up in the least likely places; be on guard always. God is the Wonderful Counselor; he will divulge his plans for you. Be available, and you will hear from God.

> Be on your guard; stand firm in the faith; be courageous;
> be strong. (1 Corinthians 16:13)

DAY

79

Watch the birds to learn about cooperation and community; they are patient, as they wait for the perfect time to fly away together. They fearlessly take off in flight, as a team, and when they rest they are in a protective pack. They have great strength and tenacity; they are adaptable, especially when they are floating in the water with winds and currents. You could learn much by watching the birds; you just have to go with the flow, and remain patient until God's perfect timing. Keep strength and tenacity forefront in your mind; when God says it is time, you must be fearless as you take flight. You will realize there is no turning back once you move ahead; you will walk into your divine purpose by being obedient to this plan.

> "Therefore go and make disciples of all nations, baptizing them in the name of the Father and of the Son and of the Holy Spirit, and teaching them to obey everything I have commanded you." (Matthew 28:19–20)

Rustic sunset

DAY
80

Allow God to dance with you, daily, like the sunlight dances with the waves. He is in you, and he will work through you when you invite God into your happenings, each and every day. This brings gladness and joy to the forefront, and keeps darkness and chaos at bay. Do this to delight in him; this is what attracts others to the light. Worldly people will not know what draws them to you, and this will bring followers everywhere you go. You will fish for people by practicing this daily routine. Ask God into your days, and marvel at the reaction you get in the world. Watch as wonders occur!

> for it is God who works in you to will and to act in order
> to fulfill his good purpose. (Philippians 2:13)

DAY
81

Practice patient perseverance, and you will walk into purpose. Keep showing up, stay alert, and be mindful of your surroundings. Watch to learn, especially in nature, and you learn God's ways. Observe how the birds cooperate; they work as a team and communicate with their cohabitants. They are a well-oiled machine. They thrive as a community, they are followers—the seagulls follow the fish; they are tenacious and yet they save their strength, resting a great deal. Once refreshed, they are able to go out and dive for fish, and they do this again and again. A daily routine, without complaint, and without demanding more, because they are content. You will be content when you rest, refresh, and then go out again. Refresh by filling up on God's love; do this daily.

> God's love has been poured out into our hearts through
> the Holy Spirit, who has been given to us. (Romans 5:5)

Do not allow the devil to get even a toehold on you; there is always something you can do to perfect your faith, and your walk. Get into the word, get into nature, get into a deep meditation; look to God for direction and counsel. Do not sit idle, with discouragement; this is a sure way to allow the enemy to lead you into despair. He is your Father, he is here to care for you, he is here loving you; look to God, in gladness and in sadness. He will show you how to keep moving forward, no matter what. Seek God first, and seek him in all things; God loves you, Child!

> Then the Lord said to Moses, "Why are you crying out
> to me? Tell the Israelites to move on." (Exodus 14:15)

DAY 83

Even when it is quiet in nature, the animals, birds and fish are there; you just cannot see them. The same is true of God; though you cannot see him, he is here. He is at hand, he is but a prayer away from you. Call out to God, and listen for his still, quiet voice; know that he is nearby and look to him with questions. Praise God, thank God, worship God, love God, rejoice in God and be with God—that is Loving God!

> Ascribe to the Lord, all you families of nations, ascribe to the Lord glory and strength. Ascribe to the Lord the glory due his name... (1 Chronicles 16:28–29)

DAY
84

Look for the Lord always, and linger with him all day; the more you do not feel like it, the more you need to connect with him. You may feel down or depressed, tired, or oppressed; this is when you need the Lord the most. Do not waste time, because time is of the essence; if you do not seek the Lord first, the enemy will seize the opportunity to take advantage of your weakness. Get in the word; meditate on God and his love, until you turn around this weakness. When you are weak, the Lord is strong; lean on him, knowing that he is holding you up in your time of need. Always come to God first, Child. This enables him to nurture you, feed you, and care for you deeply as he is your Heavenly Father.

> But he said to me, "My grace is sufficient for you, for my power is made perfect in weakness." Therefore I will boast all the more gladly about my weaknesses, so that Christ's power may rest on me. (2 Corinthians 12:9)

DAY
85

In the quiet, soft stillness of day, life is abundantly thriving; just under the surface of the glassy bay, teams of fishes are frolicking. Look beyond the rays of sun, and you will see layer after layer of heavenly clouds; take none of this for granted. It could all be gone in less time than it takes to blink. Rest easy, knowing that he is God—your protector, your encourager, and your provider. God is omniscient, but you must ask him into your days; you must keep looking to God for your every need, constantly communicating with him. Include God in everything and you will prosper, cast him aside and you will not survive. Take God at his word. These are the most important words you could ever meditate on. Now do that!

> Then I will tell them plainly, 'I never knew you. Away
> from me, you evildoers!' (Matthew 7:23)

DAY

86

Focus on God's loving gentleness, listen to his instructions, take heart when he corrects you, and really take time to look at your actions. This is how you grow. Stay in the word to get all you can for your journey here on earth; listen to good lessons, take notes, and really study the word to prepare. You are very special and you have an important role to play here; no room for error. Really concentrate on God and open yourself up to anything because nothing is impossible for you, through Jesus Christ. You will soon realize this truth.

> Don't you know that when you offer yourselves to someone as obedient slaves, you are slaves of the one you obey—whether you are slaves to sin, which leads to death, or to obedience, which leads to righteousness? (Romans 6:16)

DAY

87

Remain steadfast, remain in the light and work tirelessly toward the goal. God will give you marching orders, and he will lay a trail before you. Stay on the narrow path, follow God's voice, and do not be distracted by what others are doing. Do not be sidetracked, by the world; due diligence, full steam ahead. Wait for God to give you a word, stay in the light; you stay lit, and keep asking God to be with you all the livelong day. Ask for fresh fire, daily, and make sure you spend time with God first. Fill up on his love and rest easy, knowing that he is your Jehovah Jireh: your loving, living Father.

> Come, let us sing for joy to the Lord; let us shout aloud
> to the Rock of our salvation. (Psalm 95:1)

DAY

88

Do not get lost in the day to day, do not get too busy to look to the Lord; do not get swept up in worldly occurrences. Be grateful for everything that God provides to you, because nothing, (no one thing) is insignificant; no person is unimportant to the Lord. Treat your brethren with love, and practice long suffering with everyone you encounter. This is not easy, when you walk in the flesh. It becomes much more attainable when you strengthen your walk; look to the light, and not the world. Your loving Father sees all that you do, and all that you do not do.

> Nothing in all creation is hidden from God's sight.
> (Hebrews 4:13)

Though it is a long way to the light, you see the light when you choose to focus. Look to the light, and make your way to the light. No matter how hard it is, no matter how much the currents are against you, the winds are against you, the world is against you, you keep your eyes on the light. Let nothing deter you. Get to the light, and stay in the light; be with the light, share the light and show others how to fight their way to the light. Rejoice in the light, bask in the light and never turn away from the light; the light is the only way—"The way, the truth, and the life"!

> When Jesus spoke again to the people, he said, "I am the
> light of the world. Whoever follows me will never walk
> in darkness, but will have the light of life." (John 8:12)

Bird flying to light

DAY 90

You must follow God's commands; make no excuses to disobey: no man woman or child is worth your salvation being risked. Stay in the word; focus on God constantly, and take no breaks from being in his presence. When you seek God, continuously, he will linger with you all the livelong day. Make this your daily practice; keep in constant communication with God and you will get his counsel in everything. By staying with him, you are in God's presence; keep asking him into your days. The first thing you need to do is pray, read the word, and meditate on God and all things that are from him. When you pay close attention, you see him everywhere. See God in people who are not yet walking with him, and try to understand their pain. This helps you to deal with their issues because behind anger hides shame, hurt, fear and frustration. Treat them kindly; your job is to pull them into the light. Be obedient, beloved Child.

> Seek the Lord while he may be found; call on him while
> he is near. Let the wicked forsake their ways and the
> unrighteous their thoughts. (Isaiah 55:6–7)

DAY
91

Recognize the Lord in the tranquil, splendid, delightful day. See his work in the intricate branches of the trees, in the never ceasing waves, and in the cascading soft clouds. Feel the Lord's presence when the birds sing, when the seagulls call out, or when a fish jumps out of the water. God is everywhere—in the sky, the sea, in the sand and in the breeze. Remember him in everything you put your hands to, and it will be blessed. Call out to the Lord when you go on a journey, give thanks to him before you eat, and ask him to hold you in his loving arms while you slumber. You will be blessed by doing this and the blessings will overflow, never ceasing as long as you place the Lord first in your life on earth. Your true home is with God. He loves you, Child!

Jesus replied, "Anyone who loves me will obey my teaching. My Father will love them, and we will come to them and make our home with them." (John 14:23)

God is here, right here. Turn to him. Do it now. Do not delay, thinking, "There is always tomorrow". Tomorrow may not be here as you know it; be prepared at any time for the return of Jesus Christ. Repent of your sins and give your life to the Lord. Do this with a truly repentant heart—not for show, not for other people, and certainly not as an entry fee into heaven. Seek the Lord constantly; you will do this lovingly when you give yourself completely to the Lord. Your life will be full, and you will know a love that you have never known! You will have peace beyond understanding, and you will have joy, abundantly overflowing.

> "Enter through the narrow gate. For wide is the gate and broad is the road that leads to destruction, and many enter through it. But small is the gate and narrow the road that leads to life, and only a few find it." (Matthew 7:13–14)

DAY

93

Faithfully lay down seeds for nonbelievers and pray ceaselessly for them; obey the Lord's commands. Do not give up on prayers, seed every chance you get and water regularly. Eventually they will begin to ask questions or they will get watered elsewhere. Practice obedience in prayer, in action, in giving the lost a word from the Lord; this is brotherly love. Ignore the smirks, the sideways glances, and ignore the rolling of eyes—leave it to the Lord to lead them where he wants them. Do not hate the sinner, hate the sin. Be glad that you are removed from worldly ways; they do not understand you and your walk, they do not like it and they feel uneasy. This is good; you keep doing good.

> For he has rescued us from the dominion of darkness
> and brought us into the kingdom of the Son he loves...
> (Colossians 1:13)

DAY

94

Movement is essential to growth in the Lord. Do not waste time—work, rest, rejuvenate, go to church, pray, meditate, fill and refill. Always replenish your relationship with God, daily; ask for fresh fire, and then move out into the world to win souls for the kingdom. Show the world the love you possess by your walk; help others when you are able, lend an ear, and say something nice. Obey God's commands to you, especially when it is a personal command, as this brings you closer to the Father! Keep moving, like the waters on the earth; this is good.

> Then Jesus came to them and said, "All authority in heaven and on earth has been given to me. Therefore go and make disciples of all nations, baptizing them in the name of the Father and of the Son and of the Holy Spirit... (Matthew 28:18–19)

DAY
95

God's love is reflected in everything; if you pay attention, you will see. Look closely for God all days, in all ways; you will watch his love magnify exponentially. Go out into this dark and dying world; share God's love, spread his joy and help the new children walking with God to find their way. Help herd the lost onto the narrow path, like wayward sheep; go be like a shepherd. Get others to the light, and watch it magnify before your very eyes. That is the miracle at work in your life. Go out and share God's love with the world!

> Then I saw another angel flying in midair, and he had the eternal gospel to proclaim to those who live on the earth—to every nation, tribe, language and people. He said in a loud voice, "Fear God and give him glory, because the hour of his judgment has come. Worship him who made the heavens, the earth, the sea and the springs of water." (Revelation 14:6–7)

DAY
96

When you do not seek the light, it still shimmers on the horizon; however, the light recedes. Seek the light, every moment of every single day; in this practice you are delivered from the darkness. Watch the light grow bigger and bigger, with every breath you breathe. The Son of man brings light to your days. Seek his loving face, and rejoice (in knowing) that you are a miraculous creation waiting for your God-given destiny to come to fruition. God's will be done. Ask God to make his will your will, and ask daily. Obey his commands, especially individual commands. You only hear God's voice when you get into his presence alone, daily, with no distractions. Protect this time like it is gold and you are at war with an enemy who wants to take the spoils, because you are at war. Do not let anyone or anything take this from you; your salvation is at stake. Be with God, know God, love God, and share your love of God with the world—that is a command.

> "because of the tender mercy of our God, by which the rising sun will come to us from heaven to shine on those living in darkness and in the shadow of death, to guide our feet into the path of peace." (Luke 1:78–79)

DAY 97

Though it is cloudy out, the sun is right behind the clouds. Keep practicing faith, knowing that the sun will return; more importantly, the Son of man will return. Be sure you are ready for the second coming of Jesus Christ. Help others to prepare as much as you are able. Testify, witness, and be good to the lost; this is brotherly love. This is more necessary than ever in time right now. Look around you at this dark and dying world; you will see the lost all around you. They do not know what they are doing when they mock and scorn you. Love them anyway, like God loved you, even while you were in the darkest crevices of your life. Try to pull them to the light; never give up. Do not allow frustration to creep in, nor lose interest in helping the lost ones. They are comfortable there, the same as you were. It takes time, this is time put to valuable use; do not lose heart, stay the course—this is true brotherly love!

> 'to open their eyes and turn them from darkness to light,
> and from the power of Satan to God...' (Acts 26:18)

Do not wait too long to seek the Lord; the longer you wait, the harder it will be. Look around you at all the clutter of the world. The rulers of the darkness are trying, and succeeding, in piling darkness on top of the light. For now. The narrow path is increasingly more and more difficult to find, like a path through the forest, carved out centuries ago that is now overgrown by thorns and foliage. This is why it is paramount to stay on the path; once you arrive, if you stray off of the path it is very difficult to find your way back. The evil forces will do everything they can to keep you away from the light. You must seek God with an earnest heart, and you must be really ready to forgive others, if you want to find your way back. Better to never stray. Your Father wants you with him, where you belong. Stay on the narrow path, under the covering of the Lord.

> In him we have redemption through his blood, the forgiveness of sins, in accordance with the riches of God's grace that he lavished on us. (Ephesians 1:7–8)

DAY
99

You keep being obedient; keep seeking Christ and following his ways. He will peel off layer after layer of dead ends. You are a new creation; you will become more and more like Christ the more you invest time being with him and reaching for him in everything. Be with the Lord—read the truth, practice his teachings, and look to the Lord with gladness. Look to the Lord for guidance, counseling, and healing; rejoice that you are no longer wandering. You are with the good shepherd; stay where you belong. Under Christ's covering.

> The Lord is good, a refuge in times of trouble. He cares
> for those who trust in him… (Nahum 1:7)

DAY

100

You must be careful not to become haughty because God loves you. He loves all of his children; remember to love your neighbor as yourself. Do not put yourself first, or above anyone in any way; take the best and give it away, take the last in everything. If that means none for you, so be it; you will be provided for, and you must not fear lack. This is what the enemy wants—fear, indecisiveness, and a poverty mindset; do not fall victim to his schemes. Do not fall into gossiping, backbiting, or bickering; this is foolish, it wastes precious time, wastes resources and it depletes the fire within you. Do not let the enemy win, especially in this area. Do not be jealous or envious of anyone, for anything, at any time; you know how this feels when it is done to you. Rejoice for your brothers and sisters, when you see their walk manifested; they will also rejoice with you.

> Finally, brothers and sisters, rejoice! Strive for full restoration, encourage one another, be of one mind, live in peace. (2 Corinthians 13:11)

DAY
101

Do not think; just sit still and enjoy being with God. The rippling ringlet waves in the bay are like multitudes of heartbeats, beating to the rhythm of life. Life abounds in this season. Look around and experience all the beauty that God has placed at your doorstep. Do not take it for granted, not even for a moment; it could be swept away in the blink of an eye. Shameful, those that do not open their eyes to see, nor their ears to hear, nor their hearts to receive the treasures that God has bestowed upon his children. They need to turn to Jesus, swiftly, to have life in the light. It is up to you to teach them how to get out of the dark places they have come to adore; this is your assignment. Sit and be with God, with no thoughts of the world. Just be with God. This is where you belong!

> if my people, who are called by my name, will humble themselves and pray and seek my face and turn from their wicked ways, then I will hear from heaven, and I will forgive their sin and will heal their land. (2 Chronicles 7:14)

When you are walking with the Lord, you will be calm like never before. Though you are as calm as a smooth lake on a windless day, just like there is energy in the lake (created by God's creatures), you too are filled with his energy. The Holy Spirit resides in you and thrives within you. This is the way to accomplish greatness—to be composed with a calmness that exudes from you, (that causes those around you to also feel calm), yet to have the robustness to conquer mountains, when God moves you in the name of Jesus. Be still and know that he is God. He will give you rest and he will give you marching orders. Be fearless and keep walking in faith. Ask God to perfect your faith and your walk, ask for God's will to be your will, ask God for clarity. He will answer. Be available to meditate on God, and his commands, and you will move closer to walking out the divine purpose that God created you for, Little One. You are mighty in God.

> And this is love: that we walk in obedience to his commands. (2 John 1:6)

DAY

103

The sun shimmers on the bay, like the Lord's love shimmers on your soul. Feel his love deep inside. Get to know the Lord by paying particular attention to all of the beauty that surrounds you each day. You see God all the time, in every corner of your life, if you would but recognize what is passing before your very eyes—the birds, the trees, the grass, the breeze. You cannot see the breeze but you see it moving leaves, bushes, waves, and even blades of grass. You could get lost in the beauty. Allow it to transfix your mind: this enables you to stay still and be with God. In his presence, you will learn to block out everything else. God will teach you, when you yearn for him and his ways; you will have a peace that defies explanation. You will know a love that is otherworldly. Strive to be in God's presence each moment of each new day. Begin your days with God, and linger.

> The Lord replied, "My Presence will go with you, and
> I will give you rest." (Exodus 33:14)

Birds work together like brothers; they go out in teams to fish, they fly in unison as one and they are protected by being one, in a pack or flock. They do not have ego getting in the way, nor competition, nor bickering. They depend on each other for survival; they may have a pecking order but they keep peace, knowing that their survival depends on them working together. Man could learn much by observing the habits of a flock of birds. God created animals for our pleasure, and they are also an example to us; pay heed to the way they co-exist, and learn.

> Even the stork in the sky knows her appointed seasons,
> and the dove, the swift and the thrush observe the time
> of their migration. (Jeremiah 8:7)

DAY
105

Be sure that you know how to find God, always; there may be a time in your life that you cannot seek him in nature, as may have been your habit. Know God so well that you feel his presence when you close your eyes; feel God in the pavement, in the concrete and the buildings that surround you in cities. The world as you know it is going to change beyond recognition; it will happen in the blink of an eye, so you need to be able to find God in the bleakest of conditions. It is important to see the light behind the gray, dismal conditions that will soon be the world you reside in; you will still be able to find God and show others how to find him. It will seem as if God is gone, but you already know that he is still behind the clouds and behind the walls of rain; God is beneath the gray, bottomless oceans. The light is still there, it is just going to take a lot more effort to find the Lord—The Father of lights!

> God is our refuge and strength, an ever-present help
> in trouble. Therefore we will not fear, though the earth
> give way and the mountains fall into the heart of the
> sea... (Psalm 46:1–2)

Do not allow the enemy to get ahold of your mind; if you see him trying to infiltrate, you must immediately seek the Lord. This is the only way to protect yourself; be diligent, and by immediately seeking the Lord, (at first light) you get in front of the enemy. Make this your daily practice; do not be swayed in another direction, nor selfishly go into worldly habits. This is how you grow closer to God and strengthen your walk. You know your weaknesses, you know your downfalls, but so does the enemy and he will stop at nothing to destroy you. He will steal your testimony; he will take you off of the narrow path that leads to your purpose. Do not let him take away your purpose, as this leads to disease. Dis-ease makes you depressed and that is not the Lord's intention for your life on earth. God's will for your life is for you to share his love and to show others how to really love him, and for them to then share his love. Do this and you will see vast changes in your life, Child. Serve the Lord and you will have many miles on your feet. Get ready!

> And how can anyone preach unless they are sent? As it is written: "How beautiful are the feet of those who bring good news!" (Romans 10:15)

DAY 107

Steady, easy, no worries; rest easy knowing that God is here. You are never alone; do not take for granted the Lord's presence. Take hold of the thoughts the enemy tries to use to capsize you; do not allow this negativity. This is backward thinking and you must leave the "old man" in the grave, where he belongs. Be present of your surroundings, and accept God's love in animals and nature. Nothing should escape you; the wind, the wheat, the grass, the breeze, and the sunlight dancing on the waves. The geese, the seagulls, a stray cat and deer all speak to the fact that God cares for all living creatures. They are at peace, and you also could choose peace. Relax, and luxuriate in knowing that God is looking after your every need. He is your loving Father.

"I have been crucified with Christ and I no longer live,
but Christ lives in me." (Galatians 2:20)

Light meets Dark

DAY
108

There is more to it than meets the eye; do not make the mistake of thinking that you know what God has for you, or anyone else. He used a twelve year old boy to take down a giant, and then he made him a king. Everyone overlooked him, including his earthly father; you too have been overlooked. The Lord has a great plan for your life, and the same is true of your brothers and sisters; you could help them to walk into their purpose. This is your job, to use the zeal that God created in you and share the joy. Teach others how to light the fire within, and keep it lit. Your brother needs this more than ever now, and God will teach you how to bring the fire out in him. Be obedient and commit to this with heartfelt abandon. What you do for the least, you do for the Lord. This is Philadelphia, (brotherly love), this is very good. The Lord loves you and you show your love for him by truly loving your brother.

> For we are God's handiwork, created in Christ Jesus to do good works, which God prepared in advance for us to do. (Ephesians 2:10)

DAY

109

When you really seek the light, you will surely see it lingering just beyond the clouds. Even on the bleakest of days, you feel the light; and you sense the presence of the Lord when you awaken your senses. Exhilarating, is the person that makes it their life's goal to be with God; to be one with him every waking moment. This is the way that you become disciples, by making everything in your life about your walk with the Lord. Delight in this time on earth, do everything you can to please him, and you will have joy overflowing. People will begin to notice, more and more, as time marches on; this is pleasing to the Lord. You want to be a good child, you take great pleasure in being good; you will move forward in knowledge, in Philadelphia (brotherly love), and in perfecting your walk as you continue seeking the Father. Seek Christ's ways; this is exactly why you were placed on earth, Child. Look to the Lord for instruction, and stay obedient. You are shining for God; you see the sun just beyond the gray clouds, and that is a gift. Your heart grows more like Christ's, and as you continue to focus on the light you will begin to walk others into the Lord's light!

> "No one lights a lamp and puts it in a place where it
> will be hidden, or under a bowl. Instead they put it on
> its stand, so that those who come in may see the light."
> (Luke 11:33–34)

DAY 110

Rest with the assurances that God will always provide for you; he is God, your Father. He watches over you all the livelong day; he is nurturing you every moment. As long as you look to the Lord (and him only), for your needs, desires, hopes, and dreams, God will answer you, in his perfect timing. You may not always get what you think you want, and not when you want it, but God knows your heart better than you do, and he knows the plans he has for your life. The Lord knows the gifts that he has given you from time immemorial; he knows the gifts that you will soon develop, gifts that you have never even dreamed of. These gifts will be used mightily for the Kingdom. Be willing, be obedient, be available, be faithful; you will be amazed, and others will be dumbfounded, at your rewards. And that is just in this realm; words cannot explain, nor could humans comprehend, the rewards that await you in heaven. Your heart is pure; you do not do it for rewards, you do it for the love of your neighbor. As you become more Christ-like in your walk, you will do more and more, without even realizing that you are doing something substantial. It will seem small to you, but it is big; your presence could change a person's perspective, their day, their life—this is Christ in you. He will use you to save people from harming themselves, or even taking their own life. Keep moving forward, and stay lit; this is how you are used to impact others. You allow them to see Christ in you; the Holy Spirit shines, shines, shines through you, Child!

> To them God has chosen to make known among the Gentiles the glorious riches of this mystery, which is Christ in you, the hope of glory. (Colossians 1:27)

DAY
111

You must fight to stay in the light; there are bands of darkness trying to envelop you. Stay the course, and as soon as you find yourself drifting, you must course-correct. Get in the word, seek the Lord, and you get in the light. Do not ever take the light for granted; if you wander into darkness, you get back into the light, at all cost. The further you go adrift, the harder it is to find your way back. Don't waste valuable time; stay the course, stay out of darkness, and bask in the light. The light is where you find Jesus and his unyielding love. Here resides Everlasting Life!

> "Truly I tell you," Jesus said to them, "no one who has left home or wife or brothers or sisters or parents or children for the sake of the kingdom of God will fail to receive many times as much in this age, and in the age to come eternal life." (Luke 18:29–30)

DAY

112

Still, peaceful, quiet is what you find when you sit in God's presence. You are able to tap into your soul. You need this as a daily experience, to stay firmly grounded in God's love. The world offers too many distractions, and does not provide food. The word is where you go to be fed. You make sure to get fed every day, until you are overflowing; then you begin to see that the word will come out, naturally, as you interact with people in the world. Holy Spirit speaks through you to unbelievers; this is how God uses you to bring them to the light. You will be used more and more as you make the word alive in your life, and as you get into the word, diligently. The word does take on life; it becomes as flesh. Delight in the word, in being in God's presence, and in learning as much as you can, swiftly. Continue to be in love with God; you will grow up lightning fast, dear Child. You stay on the path; do not look left or right. You are soon to know exactly what the Lord has for you. Be ready for anything!

> They triumphed over him by the blood of the Lamb and
> by the word of their testimony; they did not love their
> lives so much as to shrink from death. (Revelation 12:11)

You must stand strong, knowing that God is always with you, as long as you invite him in. Invite God into every aspect of your life; make no decisions without first seeking him and his will. This is how you walk into God's perfect plan for your life; no shortcuts, you want to be in God's will. You must seek him in every moment, no matter where you are or what the situation, and remain steadfast. Do not look right or left; look to the Lord, only, and rest in knowing that he has you covered.

> He will cover you with his feathers, and under his wings
> you will find refuge… (Psalm 91:4)

DAY
114

Sparkling water, a lone seagull, and peace beyond measure (or understanding); feel the presence of the Lord: the calm, quiet, tranquility of the ages. No matter what else is going on in the world, as long as you stay fixed on the Lord, (on his positive energy, and on Holy Spirit flowing through you), and you stay fixed on the feeling of peace, you will be still. You are cocooned in God's love; this is his covering—you are protected. Why would you choose anything else, in this life? Slow down, now stop; stop everything. Be still, and know that he is God. When you are willing to learn, God will teach you. Come on this journey, now!

> Those who are wise will shine like the brightness of the
> heavens, and those who lead many to righteousness, like
> the stars for ever and ever. (Daniel 12:3)

DAY
115

When you fully place yourself in God's hands, you will begin smoothly gliding through life; completely opposite the bumpy roads you used to travel. Keep your eyes on him, and you will travail the storms that will always surface when you least expect them. You will find help in the least likely places; discount no one at any time. God uses people for things they do not even know they are capable of, because without him, they are incapable. Remember, you will get gifts and more gifts. These gifts will amaze you at times. Stay tuned into God and his commands; be obedient, be faithful and stay focused on loving the Lord, and on all of his ways. The rest will follow, as you walk into your purpose; then you will share Philadelphia with the world—in the name above all names, Jesus!

> Through him we received grace and apostleship to call
> all the Gentiles to the obedience that comes from faith
> for his name's sake. (Romans 1:5)

DAY

116

As you move forward (toward purpose), you will find that it has become effortless. You are in the hands of the Lord, knowing that you can trust your Father to guide and protect you. As you perfect your faith, you will walk into greater use for the kingdom. Walk in faith, and you will make yourself available for more works; this is very good. Look at the animals—they place themselves in God's hands, without fear; they know that the Lord looks after them, and they never even have to think about it. They operate on instinct, pure instinct. You follow suit, and operate on pure instinct; then watch your worries melt away. Watch your life become much less complicated; now, walk into divine purpose.

> They will be like a tree planted by the water that sends out its roots by the stream. It does not fear when heat comes; its leaves are always green. (Jeremiah 17:8)

Stand steadfast, unwavering in your belief; you know that God is your Father, he who cares for your every need, every moment of each new day. The enemy wants you to feel useless, unproductive; he wants to ensure that you will not produce fruit. You know that these are lies, meant to deceive you, to take you off course, to defeat you. Do not believe for a moment that the enemy is right. Look to the Lord for sustenance, and know that you do belong when the enemy tells you that you belong to no one anymore. This is a season where you are with the Lord; this is to grow you up, and you will develop a total dependency on him. You belong to God, God alone, and this is freeing. You will know as the days' progress why this is so important now, dear Child. Your Father has a plan. You are productive, and you will bear much fruit!

> This is to my Father's glory, that you bear much fruit, showing yourselves to be my disciples. (John 15:8)

DAY
118

Do not go around with your head down, looking for something to be downtrodden about. Go out of your way to be kind, especially when you do not feel like it.

> Be kind and compassionate to one another, forgiving each other, just as in Christ God forgave you. (Ephesians 4:32)

This will lift your spirit, and in time you will feel your troubles slide off of your shoulders. When you look for trouble, you will surely find it; and if you are determined to shake it off, you will find the light lingering around every corner. You will find favor, where you least expect it; leave no stone unturned, lest you sweep away favor like the dust. Be grateful for everything, no matter how inconsequential it seems to be. Nothing is too small to be appreciative of. Be grateful with little, and with much. You keep smiling, no matter what you come up against. Light will always prevail over darkness!

> The light shines in the darkness, and the darkness has not overcome it. (John 1:5)

DAY
119

Be still and experience the beauty all around you; do not fall victim to the enemy's snare, to look at what is missing from your life. Do not look back; that is a ploy to make you suffer. Do not think of things lost, from days gone by. Focus on what you can do for God's kingdom, in the here and now; do not take your eyes off of God, not even for a moment. Look to the Lord, with gladness in your heart, for taking you out of your imprisonment. Look forward to each new day, with a zest for life and a twinkle in your eyes. This is detected by the lost and lonely; they begin to look to you for answers, as they struggle with their bonds. You must be clear of these hindrances. Get ready to draw others to the light. Now, go forth and shine!

> In the same way, let your light shine before others, that they may see your good deeds and glorify your Father in heaven. (Matthew 5:16)

DAY
120

In your deepest parts, you know the Lord. In your longing to keep up in the world, you go off course; you drift further and further away from what you know is right. Return to the Lord by quieting your mind, by sitting with him awhile, and by reflecting on God's word. You must seek to know him by being in the word constantly, and strive to know God better. Stay in nature, and observe how the animals go about their days; sit and focus on them. You will see that they take care of their needs—like feeding and cleansing themselves—then they relax into the loving arms of the Lord, knowing that their Father cares for them. This allows them to be carefree. When you see them, you see God's love. A bird sings with delight; he is not sullen because he thinks he is missing out on something better. Be in the Lord's presence, and be gleeful.

> Therefore, "they are before the throne of God and
> serve him day and night in his temple; and he who
> sits on the throne will shelter them with his presence."
> (Revelation 7:15)

DAY
121

You must keep walking; keep moving forward, with faith, knowing that no matter how gloomy your circumstances may appear, God is with you. Keep walking toward your destiny, the purpose God created you for, and know that he has goodness and glory in store for you, Child. Do not look at circumstances, look only to God. Move forward, through the clouds and straight into the light. The light shines brighter, every moment that you exist for God and his kingdom. You are a part of the plan for mankind. Just be faithful, and keep doing what you know is right. Put recklessness away, and strive for perfection. Holiness becomes you; continue to cast aside the unsavory, and keep doing what you know is right, and spend time basking in God's love!

> Therefore, since we have these promises, dear friends, let us purify ourselves from everything that contaminates body and spirit, perfecting holiness out of reverence for God. (2 Corinthians 7:1)

DAY

122

Though you cannot see God, he is here. When you seek the Lord with your whole mind, soul, heart and strength, you will hear from him. When you yearn to know God, he will reveal his plans for your life; sit quietly, to hear from God, and you will get instructions meant just for you. Go into the word to find the Lord. To know Jesus and his ways, (to have intimacy), you must sit alone and listen for his voice. This is how you develop a dependency on him, this is how you grow; this is how you have a truly intimate relationship with Jesus Christ!

> Since, then, you have been raised with Christ, set your
> hearts on things above, where Christ is... (Colossians 3:1)

DAY
123

Pay close attention to everything; the Lord shows up in many ways. He is all around you, constantly, especially when you seek his presence. It could be as simple as a trickle in a stream, a rushing river, or a gigantic wave; it could be a sweet puppy, a ladybug in the dead of winter, or a seagull asking you for food. Pay attention to all the signs and wonders that God bestows upon you. Not one thing is too small to be considered a blessing—the person in traffic who is kind, or the least likely person that responds in kind when you wish them blessings from God. This is the kind of favor you would get all the time if you would but ask. The tow truck that arrives lightning fast, or the call center operator who goes above and beyond: that is God's favor, executed by man. You keep asking for favor and see what God does for you, Child. You, in turn, bless others, and shower them with favor.

> "Give, and it will be given to you. A good measure,
> pressed down, shaken together and running over, will
> be poured into your lap." (Luke 6:38)

Always appreciate those in service; they are everywhere, and no service is too small for you to show your appreciation with a monetary blessing. Remember, what you do for the least, you do for the Lord. Stay as loving as you are today and allow nothing, nor anyone, to dim your spirit.

Do not quench the Spirit. (1 Thessalonians 5:19)

DAY
124

Though you cannot see him, God is here. Talk to him; he is listening. God is your Father, your Counselor, your healer and your provider— he is everything. Bring everything to the Lord and do not be afraid to speak to him, about whatever is troubling you. He knows your heart, better than you know it yourself. When you open yourself up to him, you allow God to speak to your heart. You want to be in his presence daily, constantly, to get this counsel, to have this personal relationship, and to grow to be nourished and fulfilled. There are no shortcuts; show up, seek the Lord, spend time with him, (without placing restrictions on the time you have with him), and you will soon discover you do not function well without this time to fill up on God's love. Pay heed to this instruction and prosper, Child.

"Whether it is favorable or unfavorable, we will obey the Lord our God..." (Jeremiah 42:6)

In the still, quiet, softness of the day, feel God's love. He beckons you to spend time alone with him. Learn God's ways; they are higher than your ways. You cannot imagine the wonderful things that God has in store for you, Child. You must simply take the time to be aware of the Lord, and stand still in his presence. This is the only way to receive God's personal commands for you, and to get his instructions. This drives you straight into the destiny for which God created you. Be in the word, be mindful of all that you do; make sure that you seek the Lord's counsel in everything. You will begin to do this naturally, without thought; it is first nature, not second nature. God created you for purpose; sit with him in the quiet, softness of this day, and listen for his voice. You will be amazed.

> Many, Lord my God, are the wonders you have done,
> the things you planned for us. None can compare with
> you; were I to speak and tell of your deeds, they would
> be too many to declare. (Psalm 40:5)

Speck of Light

DAY 126

In the silent, stillness of the day rests security; acknowledge this, knowing that your Father is always in control. You will go through trials and tribulations. God is always with you. Look to him, each day, especially in your darkest hours; though it is dark now, the sun always returns. You know that Jesus will return soon, Child. Be content in knowing that the world you know will not exist much longer; you will be in paradise before you know it.

> Whoever has ears, let them hear what the Spirit says to the churches. To the one who is victorious, I will give the right to eat from the tree of life, which is in the paradise of God. (Revelation 2:7)

DAY
127

Do not try too hard, striving to make things happen in the world. Relax, and watch the Lord work in your life, on your behalf. When you make room for God, you will not hinder his plan for your life. If you try to make things happen your way, you do not leave room for him. You must trust in the Lord—body, mind, and spirit, to see the harvest that he has prepared for you, Child. You do not want to miss out on the bountiful blessings because of being stubbornly stuck in your ways. God's ways are higher than your ways; let him care for you as a good Father. Sit back, and watch as miracles abound and be sure that you share the testimonies at work in your life, for being God's obedient servant. Make sure that you are a bondsman to Christ. This is true prosperity.

Whoever serves me must follow me; and where I am,
my servant also will be. (John 12:26)

When birds fly, they live in faith. They do not sit and ponder if they can do it; they inherently know that their Father gave them amazing abilities. The seagulls do not sulk, wondering if there will be enough fish for dinner; they know, with their entire being, that all their needs are supplied in abundance. You are much higher than birds, and yet you wonder where your needs are to be met. You complain if it is not done exactly your way—you squabble and fight to get the best for yourself, with no regard for your brother. You must begin to really live as Christ-like as possible, faith to faith; do not give the enemy the benefit of knowing that you doubt your Creator, that you have feelings of lack, or that you are complaining. The enemy wants to create discord with your brethren, and he is trying to drive a wedge between you and your Father. Do not allow this; God knows all of your needs and he knows when, how, and what to provide for you. Do not make the mistake of trying to be God. Rest, knowing that God has all of your needs, to be provided (in the perfect time), in abundance. The harvest is coming, in due season. Until then, focus on God, and on his ways, his commands, and especially his instructions to you personally.

> Let us not become weary in doing good, for at the proper time we will reap a harvest if we do not give up. (Galatians 6:9)

DAY

129

The Lord supplies your every need, and he also tells you what you are not in need of; you must obey when he instructs you to leave something you feel, in the flesh, that you need. This is obedience. Look to God in all things, and he will show you your true needs. You must not live in the flesh; this will cause gluttony. You seek the Lord, constantly; this prevents the enemy taking charge of your life. If you do not seek God's counsel, in everything, you will fall into the enemy's snare. God will provide your spiritual, physical, and mental nourishment, but you must keep asking him into your days, Child.

> Rather, clothe yourselves with the Lord Jesus Christ, and do not think about how to gratify the desires of the flesh. (Romans 13:14)

DAY
130

Just as the waves are constantly moving forward, so must you. And, like the waves, you shall surely reach your destination. You will have the energy to complete the tasks set before you, if you continue to ask God for fresh fire. The tide is low and then high, and in the same fashion, you must ask God to fill and refill you. When you pour out love, it diminishes your energy more than you know. For this reason, you need to fill up with God's love. The Lord will send people to pray over you and this provides replenishment; you must also pray over anyone that you encounter who is in need. Continue to seek God, and in all things be Christ-like; these are the keys you need, to fulfill your destiny. Keep being obedient (fast and stay in prayer); you are only able to get to the next level by submitting to God. Stay alert, because the closer you get to the Lord, the stronger the attacks; go into your days knowing that you are God's child and you are the dearly beloved of him and his Son!

> Therefore, as God's chosen people, holy and dearly loved, clothe yourselves with compassion, kindness, humility, gentleness and patience. (Colossians 3:12)

DAY
131

Although stormy weather is all around you, rest in God's loving arms, knowing that he is your Father. No harm shall find you, as long as you are looking to God in everything. Hold onto what you know is right, and good, and true. Stay in the word, seek God all the livelong day, have faith and practice Philadelphia (brotherly love). When you least expect it, you will find that the storm has passed and the sun is casting rays on you again. You are basking in the delightful sunlight once again; rejoice in this light, rejoice in nature, rejoice in all the lovely creatures that God gave you to enjoy, and love them too!

Who is it that overcomes the world? Only the one who believes that Jesus is the Son of God. (1 John 5:5)

DAY
132

The birds are patient. They wait as long as it takes for their every need to be met, knowing that their Father will provide for them each day's provisions. They do not rush about, fretting and worrying; they are at ease, fully believing that their Father will send what they need and send it in abundance. They do not have concerns, they do not have worries, and they do not have "what if" thinking—"What if I do not have food for my young?", "What if I do not have enough?", "What if there is no food tomorrow?" They do not worry about the weather, or their dwellings; they know instinctively what to do in times of storms. They know where to rest their heads. They live by faith, entirely, and this is how you learn from them. You keep watch, remain patient; your provisions are always provided, as long as you look to your Father.

> And we know that in all things God works for the good
> of those who love him, who have been called according
> to his purpose. (Romans 8:28)

DAY
133

Silent tranquility is yours, when you seek the Lord; come to him when you need rest. Place your burdens on God. He will hold you up in times of trouble and sorrow; you need not look to worldly things for comfort. This is a trick of Satan, to turn you away from the Lord. This is very dangerous, and it teaches you to look elsewhere for what is your rightful inheritance. The deceit of the enemy is subtle, to lead you to vices, for comfort—whether it be gambling, or spending money, or lust of the flesh. Sit still with God for a while; he will teach you, when you have an honest desire to know him. God will teach you to depend on him entirely, for your every need; do this now, while the hour is young. Soon you will not have this ability; you wait too long and you will surely regret all the time that has passed by, without being in the Lord's presence, Child. God welcomes you, home; seek your Father!

> "I am the vine; you are the branches. If you remain in
> me and I in you, you will bear much fruit; apart from
> me you can do nothing." (John 15:5)

You keep being obedient, and always listen for the voice of the Lord; this is the well pleasing will of God. You keep looking to him, in all ways; do not look to the world. Do not worry about man, what they say or what they think; God's ways are higher than man's. You will be rewarded, for courageously and faithfully walking with the Lord. You do not look right or left; keep moving toward your God-given destiny, and you will fulfill your purpose, by staying on the path of righteousness. You will lose many things of the world, and many people too; do not let this discourage you, or take you off course. God is steering the ship, as long as you look to him constantly, in all things. Do this to be closer to the Lord; you will perfect your walk. Stay in the light. Keep your fire burning, dear Child!

> The fire must be kept burning on the altar continuously;
> it must not go out. (Leviticus 6:13)

DAY
135

Be as still and steadfast as a mighty oak; immoveable in your integrity, because of your love of the Lord. The same way the oak does not suddenly change into a pine tree, once you have taken off the "old man" and put on the "new man", you do not put back on the "old man". You must remain steadfast and solid; you are mighty because of the Holy Ghost (Spirit) inside you. Remember, when you sin you have the Holy Spirit within you, and you bring Jesus into your sin. This grieves the Lord.

> And do not grieve the Holy Spirit of God, with whom you
> were sealed for the day of redemption. (Ephesians 4:30)

Keep these things in mind, do not selfishly indulge the "old man". Leave him dead and buried; we do not play with dead things. Do not betray your faith. Do not go down that path; it is unrighteous. Beware of unrighteous activities, and stay away from even the outward appearance of evil, Child. Pay heed; you have been warned.

> He replied, "Blessed rather are those who hear the word
> of God and obey it." (Luke 11:28)

Allow the rain to relax you. Take the time to quench your thirst; the rain is a reminder to do this. Quench your thirst for the word; the word is flesh and you must refresh yourself on a constant and steady basis. You will find nourishment every single time you do this; fill up, to overflowing, on the word. Reflect, and meditate on what you are given each day.

> I am the Lord your God, who brought you up out of Egypt.
> Open wide your mouth and I will fill it. (Psalm 81:10)

God's word will not return void; ask the Lord for guidance, and you will hear from him. Ask with a grateful heart, believing that you will find your answer. God's word is alive; treat it as such. You will reap rewards that make insurmountable challenges seem inconsequential. Rely on the word, not man; look to God, not the world. Walk in the word; become more Christ-like.

> Do not conform to the pattern of this world, but be transformed by the renewing of your mind. Then you will be able to test and approve what God's will is—his good, pleasing and perfect will. (Romans 12:2)

DAY 137

You may not see God, but he is near; you may not hear God, but he is here. Do not allow the Lord's silence to discourage you. God is always listening for your voice, Child.

> The Lord is far from the wicked, but he hears the prayer
> of the righteous. (Proverbs 15:29)

Continue to seek the Lord in everything; stay in the word to hear his voice, worship, praise, fellowship and rejoice in the Lord, always. Look to God first; do not lean on your own understanding, or the enemy will use it to take you off course.

> Trust in the Lord with all your heart and lean not on
> your own understanding… (Proverbs 3:5)

Wait to hear from God; stay obedient until then. You know his voice, listen closely for your Father. Do not stray, do not grow impatient, and especially do not confuse the antagonist's voice for God's. Stay safe by knowing the voice of the Lord, and you must go to the word for confirmation. If you ever feel unsure, you must get confirmation. Stay on the path of righteousness.

> "Have I not commanded you? Be strong and courageous.
> Do not be afraid; do not be discouraged, for the Lord
> your God will be with you wherever you go." (Joshua 1:9)

DAY
138

Do not let the enemy rob you of joy; look to the future, remembering the promises that God has made to you. Only you. These promises are between you and your Father, and God's word will not return void. Remember this, when the enemy tries to set a trap for your fall. You are God's; do not forget that he brought you out of Egypt, Child. Take delight in knowing that God has plans for you. You will continue to be fruitful, as long as you are obedient and put your hands to the tasks that he has set before you. Do not let discouragement seep in; time is of the essence and there is much work to be done. Get ready for greatness; delight in knowing that your hands and feet, and your entire vessel, are for God's good works—speak with pure lips, and perfect your walk.

> "Then I will purify the lips of the peoples, that all of them may call on the name of the Lord and serve him shoulder to shoulder." (Zephaniah 3:9)

Stay in God's good and pleasing will, until you are standing in his perfect will. That happens when you fulfill the destiny that he ordained and anointed you for, Child. Stand firm, steadfast, unyielding in your beliefs, and do not let anyone sway you. Stay true to the Lord and his indisputable word. You keep speaking boldly, as you should.

> And because of my chains, most of the brothers and sisters have become confident in the Lord and dare all the more to proclaim the gospel without fear. (Philippians 1:14)

DAY

139

Although you are in pain, you must keep moving forward, and listening for the voice of God.

> Praise be to the Lord, to God our Savior, who daily
> bears our burdens. (Psalm 68:19)

He will show you the lesson. There are great lessons to be learned, through pain and hardship. You really pay attention, when you are facing situations out of your control, and really lean on God in those times. This is what you need to do: pay close attention to these lessons so that you will not have to face the pain again.

> Trust in the Lord forever, for the Lord, the Lord himself,
> is the Rock eternal. (Isaiah 26:4)

DAY

140

Keep moving forward, Child; look to the Lord for guidance and direction. Just like God turned other circumstances to good when Satan meant them for evil, he will show you the good in your pain and suffering. There is always a lesson for you, if you would but ask; look to God, in all things, and you will find answers to questions you have not even asked.

> Let us then approach God's throne of grace with confidence, so that we may receive mercy and find grace to help us in our time of need. (Hebrews 4:16)

You strive to learn and grow, and you will be amazed at what you are given; take these lessons and share them with others. That is a reward. Do not focus on the pain. Focus on God, and he will show you the gain.

> Those who know your name trust in you, for you, Lord, have never forsaken those who seek you. (Psalm 9:10)

DAY
141

As long as you do not hinder the flow, you will continue to move toward your destiny, that you were preordained for by your Heavenly Father. Your destiny involves tasks that no other human being could prevail in.

> The Lord Almighty has sworn, "Surely, as I have planned, so it will be..." (Isaiah 14:24)

You must continue moving forward, while keeping your mind fixed on God, and in all things being Christ-like. Once you realize that you will never be complete until you fulfill your God-given purpose, you will find life joyful, Child. Do not let the enemy take you off course; do not let your fellow citizens or your brethren hinder you either. Be forewarned, you may find envy in those that you felt least likely to be envious.

> A heart at peace gives life to the body, but envy rots the bones. (Proverbs 14:30)

You may find support in those that you felt were least likely to be supportive, and you will find that you and your supporters lift one another up constantly. You will exhort each other; this is very good. At other times you must look within to see how far the Lord Almighty has already brought you. Before you know it, you will be standing in God's perfect will, and that means living in your destiny. Look around, the harvest is ripe!

> Don't you have a saying, 'It's still four months until harvest'? I tell you, open your eyes and look at the fields! They are ripe for harvest. (John 4:35)

DAY

142

Let the shimmering lights, reflecting on the bay, be a constant reminder of your Father's love for you.

> This is the message we have heard from him and declare
> to you: God is light; in him there is no darkness at all.
> (1 John 1:5)

Do not ever forget that Christ Jesus left the throne for you and now you must live your life, each moment of every day, with this forefront in your mind—live life as if the Son of God will return this day!

> "Look, I am coming soon! My reward is with me, and
> I will give to each person according to what they have
> done." (Revelation 22:12)

Love your brother, as if it were only the two of you in the entire world; do not let blood bonds dictate your dealings with people. Often your blood brother is not your brethren; this does not mean that you do not love your blood brother, it means that you need to work hard to ensure that he becomes your brethren. Be sure to show the lost the way to the shimmering lights, lest they not pay heed to the fact that the Son of God gave his life for them.

> When Jesus spoke again to the people, he said, "I am the
> light of the world. Whoever follows me will never walk
> in darkness, but will have the light of life." (John 8:12)

DAY

143

You must not be afraid to go where God is sending you; know that he is always with you, as long as you seek him. Do not think too much about circumstances beyond your control, nor about worldly things. As long as your focus is on the Lord, and his ways, you will rise above your wildest expectations. Be fearless, as you go about spreading the gospel; people need to know, and whether they realize it or not, they yearn to be in truth. You have to help them out of the darkness and into the light, Child. This is your calling.

> I tell you that in the same way there will be more rejoicing in heaven over one sinner who repents than over ninety-nine righteous persons who do not need to repent. (Luke 15:7)

Yellow Streaks

DAY
144

As the days go on, know that you are closer than ever to your calling. Keep looking to God—stay in the word, study, worship, praise and fellowship; this all brings you closer to God. When you yearn for the Lord, with every cell in your body, you grow closer to him each moment of every day. This is very good; this is what he wants from you, Child. Without this desire for wisdom and righteousness, you lose the ability to ignite a desire for truth in the lost. They do not know it yet, but they are waiting for you, as they cry out in agony and despair. They are asking for an answer and you, Child, are going to be there to show them the way to the truth. The only answer. Stay on the path; do not detour, for any reason, at any time. You soon shall see your walk perfected.

> Praise be to the God and Father of our Lord Jesus Christ, who has blessed us in the heavenly realms with every spiritual blessing in Christ. For he chose us in him before the creation of the world to be holy and blameless in his sight. In love he predestined us for adoption to sonship through Jesus Christ... (Ephesians 1:3–5)

DAY

145

Although it is winter, life abounds. Life is all around you, exuberantly fulfilling the day's demands. Lest you think of sitting idle, pay attention to wildlife. The birds never waste a day, thinking, "I am bored", "I do not feel like going out today", "It is too cold", or "It is too rainy". They seize the day, they thrive in good weather and bad; they accomplish something each day of their lives. If you will observe them, you will see them feed themselves, (which is quite a difficult feat that takes vast amounts of energy and patience, as well as skill and perseverance). Then they cleanse themselves, and only after this is done do they rest. Do not sit idle in this season; accomplish your day's tasks, then rest to rejuvenate, in preparation for the next day. Do this and see how much more you are able to accomplish, Child.

> Never be lacking in zeal, but keep your spiritual fervor,
> serving the Lord. (Romans 12:11)

DAY

146

Stay in the light, and stay with the Lord. You no longer need to do what you did before; you were in sin. You were lost, and you were dying. By practicing sin, you start dying again; this is no good. You cannot afford to sin, no matter how insignificant you believe it is—sin is sin. Practice being one with God, by doing what you know is right, every day, in every way. Time is short. You must be prepared for the return of Christ. Do what you know is right, Child; when you sin, it tears you up inside. Why do this to yourself? Do only what you know is pure, and pleasing, to your Father.

> For the kingdom of God is not a matter of eating and drinking, but of righteousness, peace and joy in the Holy Spirit... (Romans 14:17)

DAY 147

No matter how dark it may seem to be, (regardless of the cloudy sky), you know that the sun will return. You must look forward, at all cost; this keeps you moving in the direction God wants you moving in—only when you keep moving is he able to use you, Child. Remain steadfast. Do not be swayed by the enemy, do not be deterred by naysayers, and do not be impressed with what others say to you; because it only matters what God says, in the interest of manifesting his plan for your life. When you look forward, and move forward, with forward thinking, you are being obedient. And you show the Lord that you are on the narrow path. Stay on the narrow path, walk upright, and walk into purpose!

> "Enter through the narrow gate. For wide is the gate and broad is the road that leads to destruction, and many enter through it. But small is the gate and narrow the road that leads to life, and only a few find it."
> (Matthew 7:13–14)

When you veer off the narrow path, it is very difficult to find your way back; you tend to get further and further into the dark forest. You may try to cut your way through the dark trees, to no avail; you may try to retrace your steps, and that does not work either. There is only one way back, look up to your Heavenly Father. Put all your trust completely in God, and ask Jesus Christ to deliver you. It takes time to find your way, even after you have submitted to the Lord; you must work very hard, with a genuine heart, and obedience. You then work at perfecting your walk by having a personal relationship with Christ Jesus. Stay on the narrow path; always look up, and not at the world, longing to be one of the lost again. You must be diligent in practicing the teachings that the Lord has lovingly provided to you.

> 'but if you return to me and obey my commands, then
> even if your exiled people are at the farthest horizon, I
> will gather them from there and bring them to the place I
> have chosen as a dwelling for my Name.' (Nehemiah 1:9)

DAY

149

Watch the animals to learn productivity; they do not sit around waiting for food to drop out of the sky, they go get their food. They build a nest if they are in need; they never sit and feel sorry for themselves, wishing that someone else would do their work. They do not argue over whose turn it is, they just make it happen. Weather does not stop them; they go out and brave the storm, without fail. They sing while they are working; they do it with joy. You need to make the same habits your routine; work with delight, rejoicing that you are able to work. And whatever you put your hands to will be blessed, when you ask your Father to direct you in your work.

> Commit to the Lord whatever you do, and he will establish your plans. (Proverbs 16:3)

DAY
150

You will be in rough waters, sometimes; you must go wherever the surf takes you. If you try to fight it, you will get washed out to sea. If you stay strong, you will be amazed at the beautiful places that God will take you. Trust in him, wholeheartedly, (without reservation), and allow God to take you where he wants you. Then see what wonderful work you will do in the name above all names: Jesus! No fears, no tears, no stress, no regrets; move forward, knowing that God has you covered. It is the only way to walk into the purpose for which God created you. You will be overwhelmed by the level you will be elevated to, when you let go and give God control over your life. This is the way it was intended to be.

> Keep his decrees and commands, which I am giving you today, so that it may go well with you and your children after you... (Deuteronomy 4:40)

DAY

151

Patient perseverance pays off. Heed the instructions of the Lord, and stay the course. Do not get impatient or angry, or decide you know a better way; that will only hinder you getting to where God wants you. You will not reap the full reward if you try to get in front of God, Child. Be sure that you hear from the Lord before doing anything that differs from your current situation. Pay heed to God's commands, especially individual commands; do not delay when you know it is from him.

> But Samuel replied: "Does the Lord delight in burnt
> offerings and sacrifices as much as in obeying the Lord?
> To obey is better than sacrifice, and to heed is better
> than the fat of rams. (1 Samuel 15:22)

You know God's voice, and you will have confirmations along the way. No fear of error, when you get confirmations to go along with his commands. Do not waste valuable time; you must act quickly to establish the new level God is positioning you in.

> and into an inheritance that can never perish, spoil or fade.
> This inheritance is kept in heaven for you... (1 Peter 1:4)

DAY

152

Be at peace, awaiting God's commands. Sit and be in the beauty that he created all around you. Feel God's love in nature, see the marvels that remind you that he is God, and treat nature with love, taking care not to disturb it. Treat every living being with love, gentleness and kindness; that is Christ-like behavior. You need to strive, each hour of each day, to perfect your walk and to be Christ-like. This pleases the Lord, and it shows him that you are maturing.

> Follow God's example, therefore, as dearly loved children and walk in the way of love, just as Christ loved us and gave himself up for us as a fragrant offering and sacrifice to God. (Ephesians 5:1–2)

When the cloak of dusk settles around you, remember God is near. Do not allow disappointment to creep in, nor depression to sneak up on you. Keep your focus on God. The Lord has his hand on your life. Be still until he moves you.

> Through him all things were made; without him nothing was made that has been made. (John 1:3)

Doing things on your own is not the way God's plans come to fruition. You must wait for him, in all things, or risk his plan for your life never seeing the light of day. You will be missing out on the wonderful destiny God prepared for you, and will constantly feel a void in your life, if you get in the way of his plan.

> If they obey and serve him, they will spend the rest of their days in prosperity and their years in contentment. (Job 36:11)

Sit, be still, and wait patiently, Child. Obey and your world will be so good, you will question if it is still on earth.

> If you listen carefully to what he says and do all that I say, I will be an enemy to your enemies and will oppose those who oppose you. (Exodus 23:22)

DAY

154

Sit still and patiently await the Lord's whisper in your ear; he will give you instructions for your life, dear Child. Trust in God; he knows exactly when and where he is going to use you. Be obedient, be loving, and be kind to everyone that you encounter on your way up, to where God is stationing you. You have many talents and they will be perfected; they will be increased as God chooses, for the purpose that he has chosen for your life. The Lord wants you to sit still and relax in his loving arms, knowing that he loves you and that he has you covered!

> For the Lord God is a sun and shield; the Lord bestows favor and honor; no good thing does he withhold from those whose walk is blameless. (Psalm 84:11)

DAY
155

Lest you forget, even for a moment, that God is our Creator—look around at all the beauty that he has placed in the world, for your enjoyment. Never take it for granted, take nothing for granted, because it will be gone in the blink of an eye if God says so. You must have gratitude and thankfulness for all things; a bed is no small thing, nor a meal, and especially not the shelter that God provides to you, nor the clothing to protect you from the elements. You must take time to show thanks and really appreciate all that God gives you, Child; you will then be much more driven to help others that have far less than you.

> Carry each other's burdens, and in this way you will fulfill the law of Christ. If anyone thinks they are something when they are not, they deceive themselves. (Galatians 6:2–3)

DAY
156

Moving water renews, it refreshes; do not forget it is living water.

> With joy you will draw water from the wells of salvation.
> (Isaiah 12:3)

Do not forget where living water comes from, Child; never forget that God provides living water and you never thirst again. May you have an unquenchable desire to know God and his word; put yourself in the presence of the Lord each and every day!

> Look to the Lord and his strength; seek his face always.
> (1 Chronicles 16:11)

Do not delay; put time with God first, put God first in everything, and not as an afterthought. Give thanks and praise for everything that God provides to you; do this with a glad heart, and not because he tells you to. Love God and this comes naturally, love God more than you love yourself or anyone else; this is a true personal relationship with the Lord.

> The righteous cry out, and the Lord hears them; he delivers them from all their troubles. The Lord is close to the brokenhearted and saves those who are crushed in spirit. (Psalm 34:17–18)

DAY
157

Be as still as the soft, velvety clouds in the sky. They do not have troubles or worries at all; they do not worry about tomorrow or what is going to happen later on. They exist for the moment. When you fully put yourself into God's hands, you too will live in the moment, Child, (with no worries). You will find a love for life, and nature, and people; this love is very freeing. This is a gift—this brings health and prosperity, and you are encouraged to share the news with others. Hold onto the feelings of peace, rest and tranquility. There is so much to learn by observing nature, sitting in nature, and truly experiencing nature. That experience is one of the reasons that God surrounds you with nature, and it shows his love for you. No matter where you are, if there is no other way to tap into nature you shall access the sky. If you are incarcerated, you have access to memories of nature. This is a blessing, and a wonderful way to heal.

> Lift up your eyes and look to the heavens: Who created all these? He who brings out the starry host one by one and calls forth each of them by name. Because of his great power and mighty strength, not one of them is missing. (Isaiah 40:26)

DAY

158

The beauty is all around you; drink it in. Always remember that your Father lovingly bestowed upon you the majestic earth, for your enjoyment. You must take care of what was given to you, Child; nourish and cherish every gift from God. Sit still awhile, and bask in the beauty. This is love.

> "The grass withers and the flowers fall, but the word of our God endures forever." You who bring good news to Zion, go up on a high mountain. You who bring good news to Jerusalem, lift up your voice with a shout, lift it up, do not be afraid; say to the towns of Judah, "Here is your God!" See, the Sovereign Lord comes with power, and he rules with a mighty arm. See, his reward is with him, and his recompense accompanies him. He tends his flock like a shepherd: He gathers the lambs in his arms and carries them close to his heart; he gently leads those that have young. (Isaiah 40:8–11)

DAY

159

Rest easy, allowing God to take you where he wants you. Do not fight him; be obedient, and lovingly adhere to his commands, both personal commands (to you) and his commandments.

> "I desire to do your will, my God; your law is within my heart." (Psalm 40:8)

When you do not fight against God, things will go well; when you do fight him, things break down. God does not want this for you. You are his beloved child; show God that you exalt him as your master, and that you are his willing bondservant. Watch with amazement where God leads you, when you fully give yourself to him.

> No longer will there be any curse. The throne of God and of the Lamb will be in the city, and his servants will serve him. (Revelation 22:3)

DAY
160

Look to the light; you know it is always near, though you may not always see it. Stay in the light, lest you fall because of leaving the light behind. You know what is right, and true, and good. You fail (yourself) and, most importantly, you fail the Lord Jesus Christ when you turn away from the light. As you already know, once you wander into the darkness it is not easy to return to the light; it is best not to ever wander, dear, Child. Keep your eyes fixed on the light; you know the light is where your Heavenly Father is to be found.

> The sun will no more be your light by day, nor will the brightness of the moon shine on you, for the Lord will be your everlasting light, and your God will be your glory. (Isaiah 60:19)

No matter how dire your circumstances, you can always call upon the Lord, your God. He is faithful to those who believe in him; he always helps those who follow him. Remember him as first your Redeemer, and then your life line; without the Lord, you are dead. Look to God in good times, and bad; never turn away from he who delivered you from your sinful nature. Stay true to the Lord, and practice what you know to be his ways. You will be mightily blessed.

> For I command you today to love the Lord your God, to walk in obedience to him, and to keep his commands, decrees and laws; then you will live and increase, and the Lord your God will bless you in the land you are entering to possess. (Deuteronomy 30:16)

Dark clouds with sun

You see God when you look into the skies; never forget that your Creator gave you abundant beauty in this world as a constant reminder of his love for you. When you begin to feel downtrodden, because of the dark world in which you exist, take time to go sit with the Lord, our God. Thank him for the glorious surroundings he has bestowed upon you, Child. You know that all good things, all true things, belong to the Lord, and he loves you so much that he shares the beauty with you. Take time to focus on the beauty all around you, from God. You will feel blessed, and you will soon see that you are blessed.

> How many are your works, Lord! In wisdom you made them all; the earth is full of your creatures. There is the sea, vast and spacious, teeming with creatures beyond number—living things both large and small. (Psalm 104:24–25)

DAY

163

There are times that the Lord will have you sit, be still, and wait. This may not be easy, but you must obey; God knows what he will accomplish in you once you comply with this command. Do not worry, but believe in his ways; do not stress out, but relax. You will soon know exactly what God is doing with you.

> Great is our Lord and mighty in power; his understanding has no limit. (Psalm 147:5)

There is a lesson in this, and when your Father gives you lessons, they are gifts. You need to recognize them as such, and give thanks to the Lord for showing you these things. Your Father loves you, Child, and his great love and generosity, mercy and grace, will fall on you when he gives you these lessons. Be grateful for the time to reflect on him and all of his ways.

> Give thanks to the Lord, for he is good. His love endures forever. Give thanks to the God of gods. His love endures forever. Give thanks to the Lord of lords: His love endures forever. (Psalm 136:1–3)

DAY

164

Be still until God moves you; be obedient and do as God says, when he says, without delay.

> So if you faithfully obey the commands I am giving you today—to love the Lord your God and to serve him with all your heart and with all your soul—then I will send rain on your land in its season… (Deuteronomy 11:13–14)

Be still until God moves you. If you try to move in your own power, you will peter out, like a sailboat when it loses wind. You must get ready to move, and in the interim, rest and refill while God has you quiet.

> Rather, it should be that of your inner self, the unfading beauty of a gentle and quiet spirit, which is of great worth in God's sight. (1 Peter 3:4)

Always listen to your Father to see what he wants from you, and as a result, you will find out what God has for you. You will have a good life as long as you adhere to God's will, and not your own; this is how you lead a purpose-driven life. You move into God's best.

> I press on toward the goal to win the prize for which God has called me heavenward in Christ Jesus. (Philippians 3:14)

DAY
165

Feel the gentle caress of God's hand upon you, as you take in the sights and sounds of nature. Lest you forget where this came from, always remember to thank your Creator. There is so much more for you when you leave this place, Child.

"For my Father's will is that everyone who looks to the Son and believes in him shall have eternal life, and I will raise them up at the last day." (John 6:40)

The sights and sounds to behold when the Son of man returns, and takes you home, are beyond anything you could ever imagine. Until then, be with God's creatures as they are here to give you peace and tranquility like you can find no other place on earth. Rest in nature, meditate on God; love him and love fellow inhabitants on earth.

> for every animal of the forest is mine, and the cattle on
> a thousand hills. I know every bird in the mountains,
> and the insects in the fields are mine. (Psalm 50:10–11)

DAY
166

Rest easy, knowing that God has you covered, especially when you're hurting, Child. Like a mother bear with her cubs, he may be unseen, but God is very close; he will attack your adversary, lightning fast, should you come into harm's way. You must keep moving forward, no matter how painful it sometimes is. The Lord knows it is easy to be discouraged, but you need to take heart and focus on him and his love. This life will be over in a whisper, and you need to do what God sent you here to do.

> For, "All people are like grass, and all their glory is like the flowers of the field; the grass withers and the flowers fall, but the word of the Lord endures forever." (1 Peter 1:24-25)

Do not get enmeshed in your pain; you are strong, and you must continue to stand firm. You are getting better at maintaining self-control, from spending time with the Lord, and time in the word; you refuse to take the bait of the enemy. This is growth. You make God proud when you show self-control; you keep up the good work. You will find that all of your growth will prove to be more than worthwhile, when you walk into your destiny.

> Therefore I do not run like someone running aimlessly; I do not fight like a boxer beating the air. No, I strike a blow to my body and make it my slave so that after I have preached to others, I myself will not be disqualified for the prize. (1 Corinthians 9:26–27)

DAY
167

Watch the dazzling light show in the bay for a reminder of God's presence; tap into his love, to be full like never before. You are complete, in the Lord's presence—no worries and no struggles, as long as you are resting in his loving embrace.

> 'You have made known to me the paths of life; you will fill me with joy in your presence.' (Acts 2:28)

Feel his love emanating from above and bask in it, knowing that you are a child of the Lord Most High. When you do this, you will experience a sense of peace and joy that is otherworldly. Allow yourself to sink into this envelope of God's best for you here on earth.

> I can do all this through him who gives me strength. (Philippians 4:13)

Nothing could even come close, no amount of money or status or power; nothing can even touch the enormously amazing gift of love that God has for you. Do not overlook this gift, Child; tap into this supernatural experience today!

> And so we know and rely on the love God has for us. God is love. Whoever lives in love lives in God, and God in them. (1 John 4:16)

DAY
168

In the darkest, stormiest waters, you will always find light if you look hard enough.

> The Lord is good, a refuge in times of trouble. He cares
> for those who trust in him… (Nahum 1:7)

You must always seek God's face, in good times and in bad times, to get through the storm. God will show you how to travail the storms, if you have patience and trust in him, Child.

> How priceless is your unfailing love, O God! People take
> refuge in the shadow of your wings. (Psalm 36:7)

Do not worry when you see the storm coming; it is after the storm that you look back at how much you have endured. You appreciate the peaceful environment you land in afterward. And you know that you are strong enough, in God, to overcome any circumstances. Head into the storm, with full assurances that God has you covered; you are more than a conqueror!

> What, then, shall we say in response to these things?
> If God is for us, who can be against us? He who did
> not spare his own Son, but gave him up for us all—
> (Romans 8:31–32)

DAY 169

The closer you grow to God, the greater the light in your life.

> While I am in the world, I am the light of the world.
> (John 9:5)

You went from darkness to shadows, from shadows to hazy, from hazy to clear, from clear to light and the light will stay ablaze, as you grow closer and more dependent on the Lord—The Father of lights! You must constantly pull yourself out of the shadows and out of the haze, into the light. The enemy is trying to get you back into the darkness that is lurking everywhere; be aware of the ploys of Satan. You must stay away from anything and anyone who threatens to pull you out of the light, Child.

> Remember, therefore, what you have received and heard; hold it fast, and repent. But if you do not wake up, I will come like a thief, and you will not know at what time I will come to you. (Revelation 3:3)

You only get to stay ablaze by continuously following the light that God provides.

> I have come into the world as a light, so that no one who believes in me should stay in darkness. (John 12:46)

The same way that the shadows drift across the landscape, as the sun prepares to set, the shadows threaten to overtake you, if you are remiss in focusing on the Lord. Do not let shadows overtake you; this is vitally important to your spiritual wellbeing. Follow the light, run after the light, and bask in the light—this is where you live with your Heavenly Father!

> His splendor was like the sunrise; rays flashed from his hand, where his power was hidden. (Habakkuk 3:4)

DAY

170

You will find, that by obeying the Lord's personal commands, you begin to more easily identify his voice. You will hear from God, more and more, by showing him that you pay heed to his commands.

> He replied, "Blessed rather are those who hear the word
> of God and obey it." (Luke 11:28)

This is how you grow, dear, Child. This is how you perfect your walk, and prepare for the purpose that God brought you into this world to accomplish—be very quiet, and listen for his instructions, especially when you are seeking an answer from him. It is best to wait for God before making any big plans for your life, like new jobs, new houses, or new mates.

> Wait for the Lord; be strong and take heart and wait for
> the Lord. (Psalm 27:14)

You want the blessings of the Lord and you want him to be pleased with you, so be diligently obedient and patient. Listen for his soft, still voice, and rejoice when you hear from your Father.

> Rejoice in the Lord and be glad, you righteous; sing, all
> you who are upright in heart! (Psalm 32:11)

DAY
171

Drift in the love of your Heavenly Father, knowing that all of your needs will be met. Know that he is the Lord—your provider, your Redeemer, your Hope.

> But seek his kingdom, and these things will be given to you as well. (Luke 12:31)

Do not allow yourself to fall into the trap of the enemy; he who wants you to believe that you are too insignificant for your Father to put any value on your life. The devil would have you believe that you are only here for your own gratification, and that there is nothing in this world for you, other than selfish ambitions to make you feel complete. The only way to have completeness is to step into your God-given purpose.

> He has saved us and called us to a holy life—not because of anything we have done but because of his own purpose and grace. This grace was given us in Christ Jesus before the beginning of time... (2 Timothy 1:9)

You do this by focusing on the Lord your God, and inviting him into every corner of your life; do this with joy, and watch what he does. Seek to magnify God's love and glorify his kingdom; you do that, and you will be well on your way to successfully fulfilling your destiny.

> But I have raised you up for this very purpose, that I might show you my power and that my name might be proclaimed in all the earth. (Exodus 9:16)

DAY

172

As long as you look to me, Child, you will be unwaveringly calm in the storms that will find you in this world. Do not allow anyone or anything to cause you to be unfettered; you are under my covering.

> "The Lord will fight for you; you need only to be still." (Exodus 14:14)

You now have a graceful approach to situations that once caused you to become rattled; the more you practice self-control, the more this becomes your natural reaction. This is Christ-like behavior.

> Fools give full vent to their rage, but the wise bring calm in the end. (Proverbs 29:11)

Keep being Christ-like, and do not take the bait of the enemy; look to God in conflicts, and he will show you his resolution. You will have peace in this practice, dear, Child; your Father is well pleased.

> Then the Lord your God will make you most prosperous in all the work of your hands and in the fruit of your womb, the young of your livestock and the crops of your land. (Deuteronomy 30:9)

DAY 173

You may only see a little bit, or maybe not at all, when you are in the middle of a storm; that is okay, because God sees all.

> For the eyes of the Lord range throughout the earth to strengthen those whose hearts are fully committed to him. (2 Chronicles 16:9)

God sees clear to the end; if you were able to see what he sees, you probably wouldn't have even ventured out into the storm. Be brave and fear nothing, because you are a child of the Lord Most High. The storm will probably get much worse before it breaks away. Just know that the worse your storm is, the harder the cleanup; however everything is new and pure once you get to the other side.

> so is my word that goes out from my mouth: It will not return to me empty, but will accomplish what I desire and achieve the purpose for which I sent it. (Isaiah 55:11)

Stay fixed on the Lord, and his plan for your life. Remember, he allowed you to enter the storm to grow your faith and to teach you to rely on him to guide you. Without him, you will not make it to the other side.

> We have escaped like a bird from the fowler's snare; the snare has been broken, and we have escaped. Our help is in the name of the Lord, the Maker of heaven and earth. (Psalm 124:7–8)

DAY 174

Allow the gentle breeze, blowing through the wheat or the trees, to be a constant reminder of your need for movement. Without movement, you lack growth. If you do not have a desire for movement, you will grow weary easily, and when you must move, this is no good. This shows the Lord that you have no drive or ambition. How will you accomplish his plan for your life, with no ambition?

> Lazy hands make for poverty, but diligent hands bring wealth. (Proverbs 10:4)

You must get yourself motivated, Child. Surely you delighted when you took your very first steps; remember when you ran your first foot race or took your first big hike to the top of a hill or a mountain? You must delight in moving physically in order for God to move you to the next level; show God your drive and enthusiasm to excel, in the name above all names—Jesus.

> Have you not heard? The Lord is the everlasting God, the Creator of the ends of the earth. He will not grow tired or weary, and his understanding no one can fathom. He gives strength to the weary and increases the power of the weak. (Isaiah 40:28–29)

DAY
175

You stand strong and upright; do not bend to the ways of the world.

> and do not give the devil a foothold. (Ephesians 4:27)

You must not break away from what you know is good and true. You will be pushed, you will be tested, and you may not come away unscathed, but hold fast to your righteousness. In this, you will please your Father—he who watches over you continuously. It is not easy for you. When you stand among the lost, they think they are like you, and although they may appear to be like you, be very aware of those that are not like you.

> " 'These people honor me with their lips, but their hearts are far from me. They worship me in vain; their teachings are merely human rules.' " (Matthew 15:8-9)

If you let down your guard, they can easily pull you into false doctrines (which is darkness); pray for them. The enemy is looking for people that have a false sense of security, and therefore they do nothing to grow with the Lord. They are sealing their destiny with the Rulers of the darkness.

> The one who does what is sinful is of the devil, because the devil has been sinning from the beginning. The reason the Son of God appeared was to destroy the devil's work. No one who is born of God will continue to sin, because God's seed remains in them; they

cannot go on sinning, because they have been born of God. This is how we know who the children of God are and who the children of the devil are: Anyone who does not do what is right is not God's child, nor is anyone who does not love their brother and sister. (1 John 3:8–10)

DAY
176

Be in harmony with your brothers and sisters, and with nonbelievers too.

> Live in harmony with one another. Do not be proud,
> but be willing to associate with people of low position.
> Do not be conceited. (Romans 12:16)

Do not have arguments, trying to convince others that they are not on the narrow path. Show them the narrow path by your righteous behavior; show them that you love them. When they want to quarrel, keep a neutral tone and always be loving.

> Be wise in the way you act toward outsiders; make the
> most of every opportunity. (Colossians 4:5)

Do not fall for the enemy's ploy to get you angry over other's gossiping about you; it matters not what other people think of you. It only matters what God thinks. Walk uprightly, and keep God pleased with you, Child.

> urging you to live lives worthy of God, who calls you
> into his kingdom and glory. (1 Thessalonians 2:12)

No matter how dreary it is, how cold it is, or how lonely you get, you know that God is here and he provides.

> The Lord will indeed give what is good, and our land
> will yield its harvest. (Psalm 85:12)

The Lord does not forget his beloved children; you are his so look to him for your needs to be met, and have faith that God will deliver. The animals always depend on their Heavenly Father, to provide for them, lest they would not be able to survive the harshest elements.

> The birds of the sky nest by the waters; they sing among
> the branches. (Psalm 104:12)

Take stock in the fact that they survive, and they thrive; you will also thrive as long as you put all of your faith in the Lord your God, he who loves you.

> so that your faith might not rest on human wisdom, but
> on God's power. (1 Corinthians 2:5)

DAY
178

You must help people whenever you are able; you do this by staying close to them and protecting them, when they need you.

> If you really keep the royal law found in Scripture, "Love your neighbor as yourself," you are doing right. (James 2:8)

Be kind to everyone that you encounter and help people every chance you get; especially, help elderly folks and children. Be very careful not to judge someone by the way they look, or how they act, or by what they wear or where they came from.

> "Do not judge, and you will not be judged. Do not condemn, and you will not be condemned. Forgive, and you will be forgiven." (Luke 6:37)

Surely you did not want to be judged for your looks, or for your clothes, or the way you acted or where you came from, while you were in darkness. Never forget where you came from, and what God has done for you; especially, do not forget how far the Lord has brought you. You were delivered, and other people will also be delivered. Rejoicing with them, beforehand, is exceptionally loving!

> "In the same way, I tell you, there is rejoicing in the presence of the angels of God over one sinner who repents." (Luke 15:10)

Things are not always as they appear to be, Child; that is one of many reasons you must not judge others.

> do not bring hastily to court, for what will you do in the
> end if your neighbor puts you to shame? (Proverbs 25:8)

God judges the hearts of people; it is between that person and God the Father. You see a drunk or an addict, but to God that is his child who is suffering. It is good when you obey, and feed or clothe people such as this; although this one may have shoes on his feet, he may still be in need.

> There will always be poor people in the land. Therefore I
> command you to be openhanded toward your fellow Israelites
> who are poor and needy in your land. (Deuteronomy 15:11)

You do something nice and generous for him anyway, and when you see an animal who is suffering, do your best to help him; however, remember that he belongs to the Lord. God will determine what is to become of that animal. It is God who decides when to bring him home. The same is true of people, so don't be sad when God brings his beloved home. Rejoice for them. You must know that you are going to also be with the Lord soon.

> Therefore we are always confident and know that as
> long as we are at home in the body we are away from
> the Lord. For we live by faith, not by sight. We are
> confident, I say, and would prefer to be away from the
> body and at home with the Lord. (2 Corinthians 5:6–8)

Grays and Orange

Though it may be cold, dark and bleak right now, this season will soon pass. Much more importantly, you will have a season of harvest soon, Child.

> Then he said to his disciples, "The harvest is plentiful but the workers are few." (Matthew 9:37)

You have been obedient and allowed God to soften your heart; your Father loves obedience more than hard work, and he commands you to love your brother. You have shown God the Father, again and again, that you have a heart for those less fortunate.

> The generous will themselves be blessed, for they share their food with the poor. (Proverbs 22:9)

You have grown to be truly obedient. Most people are either too afraid, or they're not fully trusting in the Lord to carry them through. He will carry the faithful ones through anything and everything. As you traverse through these bleak days, keep your eyes on the Lord. He will carry you through, and you can trust him to bring you to The Promised Land. The storm will probably get much worse before it breaks away. Just know that the worse your storm is, the harder the cleanup; however, everything is pure and new, once you get to the other side. Stay fixed on the Lord, and his plan for your life. Remember, he allowed you to enter the storm to grow your faith and to teach you!

Ask the Lord for rain in the springtime; it is the Lord who sends the thunderstorms. He gives showers of rain to all people... (Zechariah 10:1)

Rely on the Lord's teachings to guide you. Without him, you will not make it to the other side.

We have escaped like a bird from the fowler's snare; the snare has been broken, and we have escaped. Our help is in the name of the Lord, the Maker of heaven and earth. (Psalm 124:7–8)

Printed in the United States
By Bookmasters